A
Layman's
Guide to
Interpreting
the Bible

Author

Walt Henrichsen committed his life to Christ while an engineering student at a California junior college. He later attended Central College in Pella, Iowa, and Western Theological Seminary in Holland, Michigan.

Walt came in contact with The Navigators while working in the follow-up office of the San Francisco Billy Graham Crusade in 1958. After graduating from seminary, he was involved in a training program at the Navigator international headquarters in Glen Eyrie, Colorado Springs, Colorado. He then joined a Navigator ministry in Los Angeles and later went to Mexico for a Wycliffe Bible Translators jungle training camp.

He has ministered with The Navigators in Kalamazoo, Michigan, served as the southwestern regional director, was the assistant to the president for two years, directed the personnel department worldwide for the organization, and most recently was the Deputy Director of the Pacific Area Navigators.

Today Walt is working with business and professional men in the United States in a personal ministry, helping them function more effectively for Christ in the arena in which God has placed them. He, his wife, Leette, and three children live in Colorado Springs, Colorado.

Walt is the author of the bestselling book *Disciples Are Made—Not Born,* a practical instruction manual on discipleship, and *After the Sacrifice,* on the Epistle to the Hebrews (Zondervan).

To his present responsibility Walt has brought a deep and practical knowledge of the Bible as well as experience and know-how in training men to grow in their faith and reach others for Jesus Christ.

A Layman's Guide to Interpreting the Bible

Walter A. Henrichsen

ZONDERVAN PUBLISHING HOUSE
OF THE ZONDERVAN CORPORATION
GRAND RAPIDS, MICHIGAN 49506

NAVPRESS
A MINISTRY OF THE NAVIGATORS
Colorado Springs, Colorado 80901

A LAYMAN'S GUIDE TO INTERPRETING THE BIBLE

Copyright © 1976, 1978 by The Navigators
Revised and expanded edition, 1978

Library of Congress Cataloging in Publication Data

Henrichsen, Walter A
  A layman's guide to interpreting the Bible.
  1. Bible—Hermeneutics.   2.   Bible—Study.
I. Title.
BS476.H42   1979   220.6   78-27188

Navpress: ISBN 0-89109-437-7

Zondervan: ISBN 0-310-37701-3

Printed in the United States of America

The Navigators is an international, interdenominational Christian organization. Jesus Christ gave His followers a Great Commission in Matthew 28:19, "Go therefore and make disciples of all nations. . . ." The primary aim of The Navigators is to help fulfill that commission by making disciples and developing disciplemakers in every nation.

The material in this book is available in a thirteen-week video series for rental or purchase. For information write or call:
> **The International Evangelism Association**
> **Video Department**
> **P. O. Box 6883**
> **Fort Worth, Texas 76115**
> **Telephone: 817-926-8465**

83   84 / 10   9   8   7

Dedicated to
the glory of the resurrected Christ
to whom I owe my all

Contents

Foreword

A real need of this volcanic hour is a straightforward approach to biblical interpretation. We need solid food . . . not just mere crumbs. We need to learn the art of chewing . . . not just sucking on milk bottles. We need to think with some individual moral honesty . . . not continue the process of religious brainwashing. A Christian leader has said, "Christianity used to be a trumpet call to holy living, high thinking and solid Bible study; now it is a timid and apologetic invitation to a mild discussion."

Walt Henrichsen believes that the Holy Scriptures are a vital necessity and not just a speculative luxury. Hence, he pulls the plug in his book with the focus on results, not just activity in knowing God's Word.

The author is a man who sees it big, but has the capacity to keep it simple. As a theologian, pastor, Bible teacher, counselor, and father, he has placed the "cookies" down on the lower shelf where all can learn to reach and eat.

Frank E. Gaebelein has stated the case well: "Christianity is peculiarly a religion of a single book. Take away the Bible and you have destroyed the means by which God chose to present through successive ages His revelation to man. It follows, then, that knowledge of the Bible is an indispensable prerequisite for growth in the Christian life."

Biblical interpretation is more than just an intellectual game that theologians play. It opens up our lives in Christ. It is the Christian life made full. This life is to be enjoyed as we learn the basic "ground rules" and then pass them on to others. Thanks to Walt Henrichsen for taking this subject out of the libraries of the seminaries and out of the vocabulary of the "specialist," and bringing it down to where each of us is living today.

ROBERT D. FOSTER
Lost Valley Ranch

SECTION 1

How to Interpret the Bible

1 Interpretation Is for Everyone

This section has been written for those who enjoy studying the Bible and wonder if they are doing it correctly. You no doubt have heard it said, "Everyone has his own interpretation of the Bible," or, "The two things people can never agree on are religion and politics."

If such assertions are true, then Christianity is meaningless and the Bible has no message for us. If an individual can make the Bible say what he wants it to say, then the Bible cannot guide him. It is merely a weapon in his hands to support his own ideas. The Bible was not written with that purpose in mind.

Most books on the subject of biblical interpretation are quite lengthy and involved. Produced for those familiar with Hebrew,

Aramaic, and Greek, the languages in which Scripture was originally written, they seek to treat the subject in a thorough and scholarly way. For example, they contain detailed explanations of allegories, similes, metaphors, and other language uses. They explore trends in theology, such as the impact of neoorthodoxy on the church or the effect of liberalism in denying the supernatural.

This section presents basic biblical laws of interpretation in simple terms, and in so doing provides a functional tool for every Christian who wants to understand and apply Scripture.

Every person lives his life with certain basic assumptions. These assumptions vary from one situation to another. For example, if you were to fly to Japan, you would have to assume at least four things:

1. The pilot knows how to fly the aircraft.

2. The plane will arrive safely.

3. The immigration people in Japan will honor your passport.

4. You will be able to accomplish your intended purpose for going.

In our study of the laws or rules for interpreting the Bible, we must also assume certain things:

1. The Bible is authoritative.

2. The Bible contains its own laws of interpretation, which, when properly understood and applied, will yield the correct meaning to a given passage.

3. The primary aim of interpretation is to discover the author's meaning.

4. Language can communicate spiritual truth.

These assumptions will appear frequently in the principles listed in this section. Some are rules as well as assumptions and will appear as such.

These assumptions make a significant difference in the whole approach to Bible study. To study, interpret, and be able to apply the Bible *correctly* are the goals of every conscientious Christian. Before noting how these four assumptions and the subsequent principles affect the study of Scripture, it is worth noting that there are four basic parts in studying the Bible correctly. They are:

- **OBSERVATION,** which answers the question, "What do I see?" Here the Bible student approaches the text as a detective. No detail is unimportant; no stone is left unturned. Every observation is carefully listed for further thought and comparisons.

- **INTERPRETATION,** which answers the question, "What does it mean?" Here the interpreter bombards the text with questions such as, "What did these details mean to the people to whom they were given?" / "Why did he say this?" / "How will this work?" / "What is the major idea he is seeking to communicate?"

- **CORRELATION,** which answers the question, "How does this relate to the rest of what the Bible says?" The Bible student must do more than just examine individual passages. He must coordinate his study with what else the Bible says on the subject. An accurate understanding of the Bible on any subject takes into account *all* the Bible says about that subject.

- **APPLICATION,** which answers the question, "What does it mean to me?" This is the goal of the other three steps. An expert in the field said it succinctly, "Observation and interpretation without application is abortion." The Bible is God speaking. His Word demands a response. That response needs to be nothing less than obedience to the revealed will of God.

(A greater development of each of these parts may be found in SECTION III, *Improving Your Bible Study Skills.*)

These four parts of Bible study are guided by the ground rules of interpretation. The psalmist said, "I seek you with all my heart; do not let me stray from your commands. I have hidden your word in my heart that I might not sin against you" (Psalm 119:10-11). His words echo the heart cry of the dedicated Christian, whose goal is to so saturate himself with God's Word that he begins to think and react in a Godlike way. To do this, the Bible student must so familiarize himself with these ground rules that they become part of his Scripture investigation.

The rules of interpretation are divided into four categories: General, Grammatical, Historical, and Theological.

General Principles of Interpretation (Chapter 2) are principles that deal with the overall subject of interpretation. They are universal in nature rather than being limited to special considerations, which are listed in the other three sections.

Grammatical Principles of Interpretation (Chapter 3) are principles that deal with the text itself. They lay down the ground rules for understanding the words and sentences in the passage under study.

Historical Principles of Interpretation (Chapter 4) are principles that deal with the background or context in which the books of the Bible were written. Political, economic, and cultural situations are important in considering the historical aspect of your study of the Word of God.

Theological Principles of Interpretation (Chapter 5) are principles that deal with the formation of Christian doctrine. They are, of necessity, "broad" rules, for doctrine must take into consideration all that the Bible says about a given subject. Though they tend to be somewhat complicated, they are nonetheless important, for they play a profound role in shaping that body of belief you call your convictions.

2 General Principles of Interpretation

RULE ONE

Work from the assumption that the Bible is authoritative.

In matters of religion the Christian submits either consciously or unconsciously to one of the following as his ultimate authority: Tradition, Reason, or the Scriptures. The official, historical position of the Roman Catholic Church has been to make tradition the final court of appeal. The doctrine of the virgin Mary is an example. What the Bible teaches about Mary is interpreted in accordance with how the Catholic Church has traditionally viewed her.

Rationalism has occupied center stage in much of Protestantism. Liberalism and Modernism are terms coined to describe this approach. For them, the conclusion that the mind draws is the final court of appeal. What the human mind cannot accept as reasonable is rejected. Likewise, reason is left to decide what is fundamental to a faith in God. For example, a person embracing this approach may conclude that belief in the virgin birth of Christ is neither rational nor essential, and the biblical teaching can therefore be denied.

The evangelical Christian looks to the Bible as his final court of appeal. Belief in Jesus' virgin birth is embraced because the Bible teaches it. What the church has believed concerning the virgin Mary must be interpreted by the Scriptures and not vice versa.

This is not to suggest that there is no validity in each of the three forms of authority. Adherents to each of the above systems of thought would readily agree to the importance of each of the others. In case of conflict, however, the question is, which vote counts? If tradition, reason, and Scripture differ as to how to view Mary and the virgin birth of Christ, which authority is the final arbitrator? *The first law of interpretation says the Bible is the final court of appeal.*

The subject of biblical authority is often tied to the question of the inspiration of the Scriptures. A person cannot submit to the Bible as his authority if it is not the inspired Word of God. The same issue arose during the ministry of Jesus Christ on earth. He taught "as one who had authority" (Matthew 7:29). But on what was His authority based? How can we know if He truly is the Christ as He claims to be?

In answer to these probing questions, Jesus said, "If a man chooses to do God's will, he will find out whether my teaching comes from God or whether I speak on my own" (John 7:17). "If you will *do* what I ask you to do, then you will *know* if what I am saying is right or not," is what Jesus basically said. If you will *do*, then you will *know*. Doing comes before knowing. Commitment comes before knowledge. Hundreds of years ago St. Augustine put it this way, "I believe; therefore I know."

Authority has to do with the will, with obedience, and with doing. Inspiration concerns the intellect, understanding, and knowledge. The question of inspiration must follow authority. Just as it is only after you do what Jesus asks you to do that you know that He is the Christ, so also only after you have submitted yourself to the authority of the Bible and obeyed it will you know that it is the inspired Word of God.

The demand that commitment come before knowledge is not unique to the Christian faith. It is common, everyday experience for all people. In the introduction we talked about the use of assumptions. We used the illustration of going to Japan. By making those assumptions you simply made a commitment before you knew what would happen. You didn't *know* the authorities would let you into Japan. You *assumed* they would, and *committed* yourself to that assumption before you *knew*.

Expanding the illustration, let us say you go to the pilot before takeoff and inquire about the safety of the huge aircraft.

"Will it really get me to Tokyo?" you ask.

"Certainly," the captain assures you.

You probe further. "But what about the airplane that went down in the Pacific a number of months ago. Can you *guarantee* that the plane will arrive in Japan safely?"

"No," says the captain, "I can't guarantee it. But climb aboard and when we arrive (if we arrive), you will know."

That is commitment before knowledge. You are willing to commit yourself and take the risk because it is a long swim to Japan.

Therefore in Bible study you begin with the issue of authority. It and the question of inspiration which naturally follows are answered when you submit to the Word of God. You may study inspiration as a separate topic, but you only *know* the Bible to be the inspired Word of God as you place yourself under its authority.

* * *

As you seek to submit yourself to what the Scriptures say, it is important to understand that authority in the Bible is expressed in various ways.

1. *A person acts in an authoritative manner, and the passage explains whether the act is approved or disapproved.* For example, in the Garden of Eden, " 'You will not surely die,' the serpent said to the woman" (Genesis 3:4). We know this to be wrong because Adam and Eve in fact did die.

King David wanted to build a temple for God, so Nathan said to him, "Whatever you have in mind, go ahead and do it, for the Lord is with you" (2 Samuel 7:3). Nathan in an authoritative way told David what to do, but we read that his advice was wrong and that God did *not* want David to build the temple (verses 4-17).

After the Jerusalem Council (Acts 15), the Apostle Peter visited the church in Antioch of Syria and ate with the Gentiles. Paul said of Peter, "Before certain men came from James, he used to eat with the Gentiles. But when they arrived, he began to draw back and separate himself from the Gentiles because he was afraid of those who belonged to the circumcision group [Jewish Christians]" (Galatians 2:12). We know that his act of separating from Gentile Christians was wrong, for Paul rebuked him for it and then explained why it was wrong.

2. *A person acts in an authoritative manner and the passage does not indicate approval or disapproval.* In this case the action must be judged on the basis of what the rest of the Bible teaches on the subject. For example, Abraham and Sarah go to Egypt because of a famine in Canaan (Genesis 12:10-20). Fearful that Pharaoh might kill him in order to take beautiful Sarah for himself, Abraham said to his wife, "Say you are my sister, so that I will be treated well for your sake and my life will be spared because of you" (12:13). Was this a cowardly thing for Abraham to do? The passage does not say. You are left for your conclusion to your own understanding of what the rest of Scripture has to say on the subject.

You will have to decide in your mind whether Abraham was wrong in his actions or not, and this is precisely what interpreting the Bible is all about. This book will not seek to give you the "correct" interpretation, but will simply help you choose for yourself the correct basis for coming to your conclusions.

After Lot lost his wife when God destroyed Sodom and Gomorrah, he and his two daughters went to live in a cave in the mountains above Zoar. Fearful that they would never marry and thus die childless, the two daughters took matters into their own hands. On two successive nights they made their father drunk, and then they had sexual intercourse with him, one on each night. They became pregnant and bore sons, Moab and Ben-ammi, by their father (see Genesis 19:30-38).

Yet Peter said that Lot was a righteous man. "If he [God] condemned the cities of Sodom and Gomorrah by burning them to ashes, and made them an example of what is going to happen to the ungodly; and if he rescued Lot, a righteous man, who was distressed by the filthy lives of lawless men . . ." (2 Peter 2:6-7). Was what happened in the cave of Zoar a righteous act? The passage does not say. The Scriptures do, however, have a great deal to say about the kind of behavior that took place in the cave of Zoar, and the action can be judged on the basis of those many teachings.

3. *God or one of His representatives states the mind and will of God.* These are often in the form of commandments. For example, Jesus said, "A new commandment I give you: Love one another. As I have loved you, so you must love one another. All men will know that you are my disciples if you love one another" (John 13:34-35).

Some commands, however, are for immediate circumstances and are not meant to be universally applied. God said to Noah, "So make yourself an ark of cypress wood; make rooms in it and coat it with pitch inside and out" (Genesis 6:14). Jesus said to two of His disciples, "Go to the village ahead of you, and at once you will find a donkey tied there, with her colt by her. Untie them and bring them to me'' (Matthew 21:2). Because God told Noah to build an ark, it does not mean we must feel it is the will of God that we build arks; nor do we go around untying donkeys and bringing them to Jesus. The context and nature of the command indicates whether or not it is to be universally applied.

All Scripture is authoritative, but there are parts you are not to follow. You must be careful, however, not to use fancy logic to avoid doing what you know the will of God to be for you.

Secular man is drifting farther and farther from the biblical absolutes. This in turn puts pressure on the church to take a fresh approach to the biblical commands regarding such things as divorce and a wide variety of moral questions. More often than not this fresh approach is nothing more than the gross immorality that caused the fall of Sodom and Gomorrah. Such trends originate in an unwillingness to submit to the authority of the Bible.

For the Christian, the Bible is and will always remain authoritative.

RULE TWO

The Bible interprets itself; Scripture best explains Scripture.

The Bible tells us that one of the first interpreters of God's Word was the devil.

"Now the serpent was more crafty than any of the wild animals the Lord God had made. He said to the woman, 'Did God really say, "You must not eat from any tree in the garden"?' The woman said to the serpent, 'We may eat fruit from the trees in the garden, but God did say, ''You must not eat fruit from the tree that is in the middle of the garden, and you must not touch it, or you will die. 'You will not surely die,' the serpent said to the woman. 'For God knows that when you eat of it your eyes will be opened, and you will be like God, knowing good and evil' '' (Genesis 3:1-5).

Earlier God had said, "You are free to eat from any tree in the garden; but you must not eat from the tree of the knowledge of good and evil, for when you eat of it you will surely die" (Genesis 2:16-17). Satan did not deny that God said those words. Rather he twisted them, giving them a meaning they did not have. Such error takes place by omission and addition.

Omission—quoting only that part which suits you while leaving out the rest. There are two types of death in the Bible, physical and spiritual. Physical death is the separation of the soul from the body. Spiritual death is the separation of the soul from God. When God told Adam, "You will surely die" (Genesis 2:17), He was referring to both spiritual and physical death. When the serpent said to Eve, "You will not surely die" (3:4), he was purposely omitting the fact of spiritual death.

Addition—saying more than the Bible says. In her conversation with Satan, Eve quotes what God told her husband. But she adds to His Word the phrase, "And you must not touch it" (Genesis 3:3). You can twist Scripture by making it say more than it, in fact, says. Usually the motive is a desire to make God's command unreasonable and thus unworthy of being obeyed.

* * *

When you study the Bible, let it speak for itself. Neither add to it, nor subtract from it. Let the Bible be its own commentary. Compare Scripture with Scripture.

For example, Isaiah says, "Therefore the Lord himself will give you a sign: The virgin will be with child and will give birth to a son, and will call him Immanuel" (Isaiah 7:14). In Hebrew the word translated in many versions as "virgin" can actually be translated either "young woman" or "virgin." This same verse is quoted by Matthew in reference to the virgin birth of Jesus Christ (Matthew 1:23). In Greek, however, the word has only *one* meaning, "virgin." In other words, Matthew interprets the word for us and we translate Isaiah's expression as "virgin."

We will usually apply this rule to the great truths of the Bible rather than to specific verses. Such a truth is *assurance of salvation*. Individual verses can be quoted on both sides of the question of whether or not we can lose our salvation. Paul said to the Galatians, "You have fallen away from grace" (Galatians 5:4). Some Christians reading this would conclude that it is possible to lose your salvation having once obtained it.

On the other hand, Jesus said, "My sheep listen to my voice; I know them, and they follow me. I give them eternal life, and they shall never perish; no one can snatch them out of my hand. My Father, who has given them to me, is greater than all; no one can snatch them out of my Father's hand" (John 10:27-29). A thorough study of the topic of *assurance of salvation*, comparing Scripture with Scripture, however, indicates that the believer can have assurance that he is saved on the basis of the finished work of Christ.

A further application of this rule is in the use of cross-references in your Bible study. When studying a chapter or a paragraph, the context is the primary place you will look for the interpretation. Cross-references are useful, but you should try to cross-reference the *thought* of the verse rather than just a word or phrase.

For example, in studying the crucifixion of Christ from Matthew 27:27-50, you will be cross-referencing verse 35, "When they had crucified him, they divided up his clothes by casting lots." Good cross-references would include Psalm 22:18, which is the Old Testament verse quoted here. Also Mark 15:24, Luke 23:34, and John 19:23-24, all of which are references to the Crucifixion from the other Gospels. Secondary cross-references would be Joshua 7:21, 1 Kings 11:29, and Daniel 7:9, which refer to the word *clothes*.

In all of these examples the principle remains the same—let Scripture explain Scripture. The Bible will interpret itself if studied properly.

RULE THREE

Saving faith and the Holy Spirit are necessary for us to understand and properly interpret the Scriptures.

When Jesus was in Galilee by the seaside, the multitudes gathered around Him, drinking in His incredible words as He explained to them the mysteries of the kingdom of heaven. He finished the parable of the sower with these words, "He who has ears, let him hear" (Matthew 13:9). Jesus then interpreted the parable only to His disciples with this explanation: "For this people's heart has become calloused; they hardly hear with their ears, and they have closed their eyes. Otherwise they might see with their eyes, hear with their ears, understand with their hearts and turn, and I would heal them" (Matthew 13:15).

People have two sets of eyes and ears. One set sees and hears things physically, the other spiritually. The Apostle Paul commenting on this said, "The god of this age has blinded the minds of unbelievers" (2 Corinthians 4:4). The god of this world, Satan, does his utmost to prevent people from perceiving spiritual truth.

The dedicated Christian reads a passage and its truth is self-evident to him. It is so simple and so obvious when he explains it clearly to his non-Christian friend, but that friend fails to grasp its significance. Try as he may, the Christian cannot communicate the simple truth. It is as though there is a barrier of understanding between them.

Through the years Christians have been aware of this problem. Writing to the Corinthians, Paul described it this way: "The man without the Spirit does not accept the things that come from the Spirit of God, for they are foolishness to him, and he cannot understand them, because they are spiritually discerned" (1 Corinthians 2:14).

We see a striking example of this at the raising of Lazarus from the dead. Jesus' good friend had been dead four days and decay had already set in. Friends had gathered to console Mary and Martha, the sisters of Lazarus. Then Jesus arrived. The stone was rolled away and Jesus shouted loudly, "Lazarus, come out!" (John 11:43) Still in his graveclothes, Lazarus walked out of the tomb in obedience to the command of Christ.

As John recorded this event, he said, "Therefore many of the Jews who had come to visit Mary, and had seen what Jesus did, put their faith in him. But some of them went to the Pharisees and told them what Jesus had done. Then the chief priests and the Pharisees called a meeting of the Sanhedrin" (John 11:45-47). Some saw it as it was, a miracle of God. Others viewed this same event with entirely different eyes. They saw it as a threat to their own beliefs, goals and objectives.

It is easy to stand aghast at such crass unbelief. But before we judge too harshly, we might remind ourselves that this is the result of a spiritual battle. Satan seeks to blur our spiritual vision in like manner. The Bible says, "We have not received the spirit of the world but the Spirit who is from God, that we may understand what God has freely given us" (1 Corinthians 2:12). We must study the Bible with a deep sense of dependence on the Holy Spirit, realizing that He is the One who "will guide you into all truth" (John 16:13).

It is possible to claim the Bible as your authority and still be spiritually blind. You may have had the experience of being approached by someone from the Jehovah's Witnesses, the Mormons, or some other cult. These people are quick to tell you that their faith is based on the Bible, but you do not have to speak with them long before you realize that they have failed to interpret the Bible properly. Rather, they have twisted its meaning to substantiate their own positions.

This problem of using the Bible as your authority while being blinded to its true meaning is not limited to the cults. Many of the worst atrocities through the centuries have been committed in the name of Christ. In the early twelfth century, in response to the church's call, thousands gathered under the banner of the cross to free the Holy Land (Palestine) from the Muslims. It was not uncommon for the zealots in these crusades (as they were called) to massacre whole communities of Jews and pagans, even impaling infants by throwing them into the air and catching them on their spears.

During the Civil War in America the Bible was used both to denounce and to support slavery. It is reported that one of Abraham Lincoln's generals said to him during the fierce conflict, "I hope God is on our side."

The president replied, "Sir, I am not half as concerned that God is on our side as I am that we are on God's side."

Seeing things from God's point of view is a ministry of the Holy Spirit to those who have not only trusted Him for salvation but for enlightenment as well. Though being a Christian is no guarantee that you will accurately interpret every passage in the Bible, it is foundational for properly understanding spiritual truth.

RULE FOUR

Interpret personal experience in the light of Scripture and not Scripture in the light of personal experience.

As you read through the New Testament, you discover that it contains two main types of literature—narrative and instructional or teaching. (Most of Revelation and parts of the Gospels can be classified as prophetic.) The narrative portions trace the life of our Lord Jesus in the four Gospels and the history of the early church in the Book of Acts. The letters or epistles are largely written to instruct members of these early churches on how to live the Christian life.

When studying the instructional portions you discover the writer does not say that because such and such a thing happened, therefore this must be true. Rather, he asserts just the opposite. Because this is true, a particular thing happened. For example, the New Testament does not teach that because Jesus rose from the dead He is therefore the Son of God. Rather, because He is the Son of God, He rose from the dead.

The events that unfold throughout the Bible are interpreted on the basis of what God states to be true and never vice versa. We do not conclude that the world was wicked because God destroyed it with a flood in the days of Noah. Rather, the Bible says that because the world was wicked God said He would destroy it and did.

Throughout the Book of Acts the narrative of what happened in the lives of first century believers unfolds. You do not draw doctrinal conclusions from these events unless they include preaching. Rather, you interpret these events in the light of the doctrinal passages. There are several instances when people in the Acts record encountered the Holy Spirit. When you analyze all the varied experiences, it becomes obvious that you cannot form doctrine from these encounters. On the Day of Pentecost Peter and the disciples spoke in tongues, and people of different language groups were all able to understand the gospel in their own languages. "Utterly amazed, they asked: 'Are not all these men who are speaking Galileans? Then how is it that each of us hears them in his own native language?'" (Acts 2:7-8).

When Peter went to Samaria to look in on the ministry of Philip, the new converts had not yet received the Holy Spirit. "Then Peter and John placed their hands on them, and they received the Holy Spirit" (Acts 8:17). There is no mention of any speaking in tongues following this occurrence.

After Paul's conversion on the road to Damascus, Ananias came to him and laid hands on him. Paul was filled with the Holy Spirit and was baptized (Acts 9:17-19).

In the city of Ephesus Paul met some men who had been baptized only with "John's baptism"—a baptism of repentance. Paul preached Jesus to them, and they believed and were baptized.

"When Paul placed his hands on them, the Holy Spirit came on them, and they spoke in tongues and prophesied" (Acts 19:6). We are not told what language these men spoke, but it probably was different from that spoken at Pentecost. The situation was different. It was most likely an unknown tongue, requiring an interpreter such as Paul mentions in his letter to the Corinthians (1 Corinthians 14).

The teaching portions of the New Testament speak about the use of tongues by believers. The significant passage on this teaching is 1 Corinthians 12–14. Note that this passage addresses itself to the use and control of tongues without mentioning the practice of tongues as in Acts. In other words, Paul says, "Here is the correct doctrine regarding tongues—make sure your own experience complies with it." He does not say that because a certain phenomenon was experienced in the church, a certain doctrinal truth may be drawn from it.

Your personal experiences—whatever they may be—must be taken to the Scriptures and interpreted. Never the other way around. "Because I have had this experience, the following must be true" is not sound procedure in interpreting the Bible.

None of this suggests that there is no value in experience. Quite the contrary. Experience attests to the validity of the doctrine. The resurrection of Jesus Christ substantiates the fact that He is the Son of God. You know that your salvation is true because of what you have experienced. But you do not form the doctrine of salvation on the basis of your experience. You take your experience to the Scriptures to find out what has taken place in your life.

We often see in the Bible that a statement is made and an experience follows to prove its validity. For example, we find the following test to see if the man claiming to be a prophet really is one: "If what a prophet proclaims in the name of the Lord does not take place or come true, that is a message the Lord has not spoken. That prophet has spoken presumptuously. Do not be afraid of him" (Deuteronomy 18:22).

Ahaziah, the son of Ahab and Jezebel, was king over Israel, the northern kingdom. Because of his sin, Elijah the prophet prophesied that he would die. King Ahaziah sent soldiers to arrest Elijah. "Elijah answered the captain, 'If I am a man of God, may fire come down from heaven and consume you and your fifty men!' Then fire fell from heaven and consumed the captain and his men" (2 Kings 1:10). Elijah's prophetic statement was followed by its fulfillment, proving that Elijah was a true prophet of God. His statement was followed by the experience.

Personal experience is an important part of the Christian life, but you must be careful to keep it in its proper place. Though you learn from experience, you do not judge the Bible on the basis of it.

It is easy to forget this in so many areas in life. For example, suppose you have had difficulty with deficit spending. The Lord speaks to you about this and you feel He would have you abolish all forms of buying on credit. You work hard, economize, and pay off all your creditors. This revolutionizes your life. You are now free from debt and convinced that you should never return to install-ment buying. Up to this point all is well.

But then you go one step further and suggest that anyone owning credit cards or buying on time is violating a biblical command. To prove your point you quote, "Let no debt remain outstanding" (Romans 13:8). You have now broken this important rule of interpretation. You have interpreted the Bible in the light of your own experience and demanded that others should follow this interpretation.

The Scriptures blend beautifully with life's experiences. The more time you spend in Bible study, the more this truth becomes imprinted in your life. It seems that the biblical authors had *you* in mind when they penned their words, so pointed and alive are the applications.

It is precisely for this reason that you must exercise care in not reversing this rule. You allow the Word of God to interpret and shape your experiences rather than interpreting Scripture from your experiences.

RULE FIVE

Biblical examples are authoritative only when supported by a command.

As you read through the Bible it becomes obvious that you are not to follow the example of every person you meet. You need not follow the example of Moses and confront the leaders of Egypt. You are not to follow the example of King David and commit adultery and murder. Nor are you to follow the example of the Apostle Peter in denying Christ.

These illustrations may seem to be oversimplified, but the Bible is full of many examples that *are* worthy of imitation. Are you not obligated to follow these? Yes, if the example illustrates a biblical command. No, if the example is not supported by such a command.

Jesus Christ is the perfect Man. If ever there is a life worth copying it is His. As we look at His perfect life, if we find it is not necessary to follow all His examples, it will logically follow that this will be true for the rest of the Bible.

Jesus wore a long robe and sandals. Usually He walked. When He did ride, it was on a donkey. He never married and never left the country of His birth (except as an infant when His parents fled to Egypt to escape from King Herod and a brief visit to Syro-Phoenicia). It becomes immediately apparent that you are not expected to follow His example in areas such as these.

For instance, to follow Jesus' example in His remaining single would mean that Christians are not to marry; yet the Bible has a great deal to say about the marital relationship, commending it highly and using it as an illustration of the whole Christ-Church relationship.

Jesus was a man of great love and compassion. You know you are to follow His example in this because He said, "A new commandment I give you: Love one another. As I have loved you, so you must love one another. All men will know that you are my disciples if you love one another" (John 13:34-35).

Examples from the life of Jesus or from the lives of His follow-ers that are *not* supported by commands do have some value:

1. *A biblical example can verify what you think the Lord is leading you to do.* You may feel, for instance, that God would have you remain single the rest of your life. Since most people marry, you may feel pressure from others in this direction. But your conviction that the Lord would have you never marry is biblically supported by the fact that Jesus never married.

2. *A biblical example can be a rich source of application for your life.* Suppose you are reading the Gospel of Mark and pause to meditate on this account, "Very early in the morning, while it was still dark, Jesus got up, left the house and went off to a solitary place, where he prayed" (Mark 1:35). After thought and prayer you feel the Lord would have you spend time with Him each day early in the morning. This would be an appropriate application and would undoubtedly benefit your spiritual life.

To take this application, however, and try to apply it to other people would be taking an example from the Bible and treating it as a command. The Scripture does command us to pray; Paul urged, "Pray continually" (1 Thessalonians 5:17). And the Bible does exhort us to spend time in the Word, "Let the Word of Christ dwell in you richly as you teach and counsel one another with all wisdom, and as you sing psalms, hymns and spiritual songs with gratitude in your hearts to God" (Colossians 3:16). No command of Scripture says that this should be done early in the morning, even though this is when Jesus did it, and may be the best time for you.

Each individual must draw his own application from those biblical examples that are not followed by a command. The com-mandments of the Bible are, of course, authoritative for all people. But biblical examples, unless supported by a command, are not.

* * *

A corollary to this principle is also true:

The believer is free to do anything that the Bible does not prohibit.

An obvious example of this principle may be seen in the present-day activities of the church. A local congregation may build a new sanctuary, develop a large Sunday School, begin a Boys Brigade work, or start a Christian day school. The Scriptures do not have examples of these, much less commands to do them, yet such actions are entirely permissible. The Bible sets boundaries on what *cannot* be done, not on what can be done. All things are lawful unless specifically prohibited.

Such a clear prohibition applies in the area of premarital and extramarital sex. Paul says that such people "will not inherit the kingdom of God" (see 1 Corinthians 6:9).

The Holy Spirit uses the Bible to guide and direct our lives. As we follow His leading and expose ourselves to the great truths of the Scriptures, we take upon ourselves more and more the character of Jesus Christ. The Bible calls this process sanctification. And in sanctification the Lord gives us great freedom—freedom in the exciting adventure of becoming Christlike.

As we study the Bible, we must exercise care that we do not restrict this freedom either for ourselves or for others. To quote the great Puritan divines of a by-gone day, "The Bible is our only rule for faith and practice."

RULE SIX

The primary purpose of the Bible is to change our lives, not increase our knowledge.

When He superintended the writing of the Bible, the Holy Spirit intended that we who read the Scriptures learn and apply what is taught. The Scriptures themselves state this as their intended purpose.

When Paul wrote his first epistle to the Corinthians, he drew from the experience of Israel during the Exodus to make his point. Israel lusted in the wilderness for things they didn't have.

Commenting on this to the church in Corinth, Paul said, "Now these things occurred as examples, to keep us from setting our hearts on evil things as they did" (1 Corinthians 10:6)

Two of the ways you can learn a lesson are through personal experiences and through the experiences of others. Some lessons in life you can learn only by living through them. But some lessons are too expenseive to learn that way. The wise person will learn them by observing the lives of others.

The unbelief of Israel during the Exodus cost that nation forty wasted years of wandering in the wilderness. Paul says to the Corinthians that God recorded this for us so that we would not make the same tragic mistakes. In a most remarkable way the Lord shows us in the pages of the Bible the failures and shortcomings (as well as the strengths) of His people so that we can learn from them. "Learn from their strengths and avoid their weaknesses," seems to be the Holy Spirit's message to us.

We must understand before we can apply, but understanding without application does not make a person godly. Satan knows the Bible well. No doubt he could pass any examination in theology offered him. He has even memorized Scripture, which he demonstrated when he quoted from the Psalms during the temptation of Jesus.

"Then Jesus was led by the Spirit into the desert to be tempted by the devil. After fasting forty days and nights, he was hungry. The tempter came to him and said, 'If you are the Son of God, tell these stones to become bread.'

"Jesus answered, 'It is written: "Man does not live on bread alone, but on every word that comes from the mouth of God."'"

"Then the devil took him to the holy city and had him stand on the highest point of the temple. 'If you are the Son of God,' he said, 'throw yourself down. For it is written: "He will command his angels concerning you, and they will lift you up in their hands, so that you will not strike your foot against a stone"'" [Psalm 91:11-12].

"Jesus answered him, 'It is also written: "Do not put the Lord your God to the test."'"

"Again, the devil took him to a very high mountain and showed him all the kingdoms of the world and their splendor. 'All this I will give you,' he said, 'if you will bow down and worship me.'

"Jesus said to him, 'Away from me, Satan! For it is written: "Worship the Lord your God, and serve him only."'" Then the devil left him, and angels came and attended him" (Matthew 4:1-11).

"Even the demons believe that—and shudder," is the way James put it (James 2:19). The Bible was not given to us so that we could be as smart as the devil; it was given to us so that we could become as holy as God. Peter has written: "He has given us his very great and precious promises, so that through them you may participate in the divine nature and escape the corruption in the world caused by evil desires" (2 Peter 1:4).

Paul advised Timothy, "All Scripture is God-breathed and is useful for teaching, rebuking, correcting and training in righteousness, so that the man of God may be thoroughly equipped for every good work" (2 Timothy 3:16-17). All Scripture was given with this end in mind—that it shape our lives. You must be careful, though, when seeking to apply "all Scripture" to remember two things. They may be stated as corollaries to this rule.

* * *

1. Some passages are not to be applied in the same way they were applied at the time they were written.

Suppose you are reading through the Book of Leviticus, seeking to make an application to your life, and you read, "These are the regulations for the guilt offering, which is most holy: The guilt offering is to be slaughtered in the place where the burnt offering is slaughtered, and its blood is to be sprinkled against the altar on all sides" (Leviticus 7:1-2). A wrong application would be to do the same thing the Old Testament priests did: offer an animal sacrifice.

The New Testament tells us that Jesus Christ "abolished in His flesh the enmity, even the law of commandments contained in ordinances" (Ephesians 2:15 KJV). You might possibly apply this Leviticus passage by purposing to reflect on how great a price the Savior paid to have every one of your sins forgiven, using the Old Testament sacrificial system as a point of reference.

The Bible offers another possible application: "Through Jesus, therefore, let us continually offer to God a sacrifice of praise—the fruit of lips that confess his name. And do not forget to do good and to share with others, for with such sacrifices God is pleased" (Hebrews 13:15-16).

2. When you apply a passage it must be in keeping with a correct interpretation.

For example, our Lord is coming down from the Mount of Transfiguration when He meets some of His disciples trying to heal an epileptic (Matthew 17:14-16). Since they are unable to do it, the boy's father turns to Jesus for help. Jesus casts out the unclean spirit and the frustrated disciples later ask why they were unable to do it. Jesus replies, "Because you have so little faith. I tell you the truth, if you have faith as small as a mustard seed, you can say to this mountain, 'Move from here to there' and it will move. Nothing will be impossible for you" (17:20).

If you were burdened for a loved one who had a terminal disease, you might read this passage, and, wanting to make an application, reason that only your lack of faith was keeping you from healing him. You try to heal him, but the person dies. So you blame yourself and think, *Maybe it is because of sin in my life that I was unable to heal him.*

Probably sin and unbelief were not your problem. You simply misinterpreted the passage. Earlier, Jesus had specifically instructed His disciples, "Heal the sick, raise the dead, cleanse those who have leprosy, drive out demons. Freely you have received, freely give'' (Matthew 10:8). They were rebuked for their lack of faith because they had been commanded by the Lord to heal and had been endowed with appropriate power to do so. God did not give such a specific command to you.

Every part of the Bible is applicable to you. Correct interpretation, however, is essential before you seek to make application. Failure to do so may lead to unnecessary misunderstanding and heartache. Take care to interpret the passage correctly, then prayerfully make the application.

RULE SEVEN

Each Christian has the right and responsibility to investigate and interpret the Word of God for himself.

This principle was one of the undergirding foundations of the Protestant Reformation in the sixteenth century. For hundreds of years, people had depended on the church to do the studying and interpreting of the Scriptures for them. There were no translations of the Bible in the language of the people. When attempts were made to produce such translations, the church strongly suppressed them.

Today there are a multitude of available translations and paraphrases, making access to the Bible easy for anyone who can read. Yet our generation seems to be producing biblically illiterate people. Even among conscientious Christians the Bible is little more than a devotional book in which to ''meet'' God. Digging for the great truths of the Bible is left for the theologians and other ''experts.'' It is as though we were returning to the days before the Reformation.

The presence of the Holy Spirit and the ability of language to communicate truth combine to give you all you need to study and interpret the Bible for yourself. In the ministry of our Lord Jesus, He rebuked the Jews of His day for their inability to understand who He was. He attributed this failure directly to their ignorance of the Scriptures. "You diligently study the Scriptures because you think that by them you possess eternal life. These are the Scriptures that testify about me" (John 5:39).

Later Jesus said that a distinguishing mark of one who is His disciple is that he "continue in My Word" (John 8:31 KJV). All through the epistles this theme is picked up and emphasized. "Let the word of Christ dwell in you richly as you teach and counsel one another with all wisdom, and as you sing psalms, hymns and spiritual songs with gratitude in your hearts to God" (Colossians 3:16), Paul admonished the believers at Colosse. To his son in the faith he put it this way, "Do your best to present yourself to God as one approved, a workman who does not need to be ashamed and who correctly handles the word of truth" (2 Timothy 2:15).

In-depth study will not always give you the answers you seek. Frequently you will encounter a truth whose depths elude you. And your mind is so constituted that it can ask more questions than it can answer. Bible study will not answer all of your questions. Answers to some questions will come later, like finding the missing piece in a jigsaw puzzle. Some will never be answered this side of heaven. An appreciation for the mysteries in the Christian faith is in itself a sign of maturity.

When your private interpretation leads you to a conclusion different from the historic meaning men of God have given to the passage, an amber light of caution should flash in your mind. Any conclusion you come to that differs from the historic evangelical position should be considered suspect. More often than not, after further study, you will find that your interpretation was in error.

If you are blessed with a pastor and Sunday School that faithfully expound the Bible, you have a rich heritage indeed. This, however, could easily lull you into relying on others to feed you rather than disciplining yourself to feed your own soul. It should not be an either/or proposition, but a both/and. You should maintain a balance between being taught by others and feeding yourself. The more skilled you become in personal Bible study, the more you will rely on your pastor as a check on how you interpreted the passage rather than as the primary source of your scriptural intake.

Even when you learn spiritual truth from the preaching of others, you are responsible for weighing this truth with what you find in your own Bible study and for forming your own convictions. This is what made the Berean Church noble in the eyes of Luke. Notice what he said about them. "Now the Bereans were of more noble character than the Thessalonians, for they received the message with great eagerness and examined the Scriptures every day to see if what Paul said was true" (Acts 17:11).

Underline the words *great eagerness*. The noble Bereans received Paul's teaching with openness and attentiveness. But they did not stop there. When Paul was through preaching, they examined "the Scriptures every day to see if what Paul said was true." What a combination! Listen attentively to the Word and then study the Bible to form your own convictions.

When you accept an idea simply because someone else tells you it is so, you short-circuit the process, even if what you are told is accurate and worthy of belief. You have believed the right thing for the wrong reason. It has not yet become your conviction. This is why so many Christians fall prey to heretical groups such as the Jehovah's Witnesses and the Mormons.

A different illustration will make the same point. A Christian friend encourages you to memorize Scripture. You do it because he tells you to do it. You have no conviction of your own that you should do it, and it is hard work. After an enthusiastic beginning you let it slip. Unfaithful in your review, you soon forget the verses you have memorized, and in discouragement you quit. Only if you are *convinced* God wants you to memorize, will you jump the hurdles of discouragement and go on to victory.

As we have already seen, God commands us to spend time with Him in the Scriptures. Scripture memory, however, is a *method* of getting into the Word. You may not necessarily be convinced of the method that others use; in that case you must go before the Lord and ask Him *how* He wants you to go about investigating and interpreting the Bible.

Five methods of studying the Bible are presented later on in Section II of this book. Further suggestions for improving your investigation of the Word of God are given in Section III.

A method is a vehicle for digging into the Word. The process of digging into Scripture and coming to your own conclusion is what changes mere beliefs into rock-ribbed convictions. Involvement in this process is not only your right as a child of God, but also your solemn responsibility.

RULE EIGHT

Church history is important but not decisive in the interpretation of Scripture.

In the introduction to this book, we compared the authority of *reason* and *tradition* to the authority of *Scripture*. Though all three authorities are important and have their proper place, reason and tradition must yield to Scripture. When there is disagreement among the three types of authority, Scripture must be the final court of appeal. It is the *final* authority.

There is a proper place for reason and tradition, and here we want to examine the place of tradition or church history. For the sake of simplicity we will equate the two.

Many doctrines considered essential by evangelicals are implied in the Scriptures. Because they are implied and not explicitly stated, there was a time when they were quite controversial. We are indebted to church history for the fact that such issues are settled.

One such doctrine is the deity of Jesus Christ, that is, that He is coeternal with the Father, that He is God. There never was a time when He was not. He is "very God of very God." This doctrine is biblical. It is taught in several places in the Bible. The prologue to the Gospel of John gives a clear example, "In the beginning was the Word, and the Word was with God, and the Word was God. . . . The Word became flesh and lived for a while among us'' (John 1:1, 14). The correct interpretation of this and other related passages came with the maturing of the church. We are indebted to church history which records what the believers of past ages hammered out on the anvil of soul-searching, scriptural investigation and debate.

* * *

A corollary to this rule is:

The church does not determine what the Bible teaches; the Bible determines what the church teaches.

The interpretations of the church have authority only insofar as they are in harmony with the teachings of the Bible as a whole. History was not meant to be decisive in the interpretation of Scripture, for there have been times when the church has not been true to the Word of God. In early medieval times it taught the celibacy of the clergy, that priests could never marry. Later medieval times exalted Mary to a position equal with God. These were determinations of the church, not the Bible. The interpretations of the church must be carefully studied and evaluated in light of what the Bible teaches.

Having voiced this caution, however, we still must not overlook the importance of church history. It can provide a check and balance for you in your own study of the Bible. Charles H. Spurgeon, the famous English preacher, is reported to have said, ''It seems odd that certain men who talk so much of what the Holy Spirit reveals to them should think so little of what He revealed to others.'' There is an important place for commentaries and the creeds in forming doctrine. God's saints of the past have a great deal to say to us today, if only we will listen.

Many evangelicals overreact by refusing to consider any source other than the Bible, and not without reason. The attack on the Word of God has been fierce these past decades. Many of the historic creeds of the church have been revised and watered down to include the philosophical biases of the day. You must be careful to maintain balance here. Learn from history and recognize its important contribution while remembering that the Bible is the final arbitrator in all matters pertaining to faith and practice.

RULE NINE

The promises of God throughout the Bible are available to the Holy Spirit for the believers of every generation.

The promises of God found in the Bible are a means by which God reveals His will to men. In saying this, we must acknowledge that claiming promises is a subjective thing. For that matter, so is using any method to determine God's will for one's life.

Many people become uneasy when biblical promises are used, partly because they are so often misused. A not-so-funny caricature of a person claiming a biblical promise shows him opening a Bible with eyes closed and placing his finger in the middle of the page. Where the finger rests is God's promise to him.

The problem is not in claiming a promise per se, but in determining the will of God. Use the same caution in claiming God's promises that you use when you determine the will of God. The Lord requires all of us to act on the basis of faith. The promises are given as a valuable tool in helping us respond properly.

Claiming the promises of God is a specific form of application. Note the emphasis that was given to application in Rule Six: *The primary purpose of the Bible is to change our lives, not increase our knowledge* (page 33). Just as it is essential that you interpret the passage properly before applying it, so also it is essential to interpret the promise properly before claiming it.

If you are not careful about what the passage says, all sorts of fanciful interpretations can follow. For example, you may desire leadership from the Lord for your life. After much prayer you claim Isaiah 30:21, "Whether you turn to the right or to the left, your ears will hear a voice behind you, saying, 'This is the way; walk in it.' " You are asking the Lord to tell you when to turn to the right and when to turn to the left. From now on you are going to get your directions straight from God, for is this not what He has promised?

As you study the context of Isaiah 30:21, you learn that the word spoken from behind you is from your teachers. From God, yes, but through your teachers. Failure to interpret the verse properly can lead you to misunderstand how God wants to lead you.

It is permissible to claim a promise outside of its historical context as long as you are true to what the passage says and means. For example, let us say you are surrounded by adverse circumstances and accused falsely. You pray, asking the Lord for guidance. He leads you to claim Exodus 14:14, "The Lord will fight for you; you need only to be still." This promise was originally given to Moses when Israel was surrounded by adverse circumstances. But with this promise God quiets your heart and you wait on Him to work things out.

The Bible gives numerous encouragements to claim the promises in this manner. Peter, exhorting his flock to a devout and holy life, said, "His divine power has given us everything we need for life and godliness through our knowledge of him who called us by his own glory and goodness. Through these he has given us his very great and precious promises, so that through them you may participate in the divine nature and escape the corruption in the world caused by evil desires" (2 Peter 1:3-4). The psalmist expressed it this way: "But the plans of the Lord stand firm forever, the purposes of his heart through all generations" (Psalm 33:11).

A proper attitude is important as you approach the promises. The Lord has given them to you to help you do His will. Yet so often people use them to try to get God to do their will. The Bible says, "Until now you have not asked for anything in my name. Ask and you will receive, and your joy will be complete" (John 16:24). Jesus Himself made that promise. You are in love with someone and want to marry that person. Or you and your spouse want a child. So you claim this promise, but don't get your wish. Why? Possibly because God did not give you that particular promise. You took it. But God is not your servant; you are His. You defeat the purpose of the promises when you make them self-serving.

A promise is God's commitment to do something, and requires your response of faith in the form of obedience. Sometimes that obedience means patiently waiting on the Lord to do what He promises. Another time it may mean launching out into the unknown or taking great risks. God's promises form the foundation for the expression of faith. Without the promise you have no basis for asking. With the promise you respond by faith. Faith is always active, never passive. As you, by faith, respond to God's promise, His will is performed and He is glorified.

Suppose you respond to the promise and it is not fulfilled? It appears that God did not do what He promised. To what conclusions can you then come? Three possibilities are:

1. *God let you down.* He failed to carry out His end of the bargain. If this is so, the Bible is not trustworthy; it is not worth following Christ; in short, the God of the Scriptures does not exist. For God Himself said, "God is not a man, that he should lie, nor a son of man, that he should change his mind. Does he speak and then not act? Does he promise and not fulfill?" (Numbers 23:19).

Though we list "God let you down" as a possible conclusion, it is in fact an impossibility. It is an impossibility because God promises He will *never* let us down. Paul was speaking to Timothy when he said, concerning the reliability of God, "He will remain faithful, for he cannot disown himself" (2 Timothy 2:13). We can rule out this possibility simply because God *always* does what He promises.

2. *You misclaimed the promise*. This is an unpleasant possibility, but a real one. If you have ever had the misfortune of claiming a promise God never intended for you to claim, don't think that you are alone. Many have done it. It usually happens when your motives become confused. Was the promise claimed with a sincere desire to do God's will and nothing else? Or was what you wanted interjected somewhere along the line?

If you felt you sought only to please God, then you should suspend judgment as to what happened. Even Paul wasn't always sure of his own motives. He said, "I care very little if I am judged by you or by any human court; indeed, I do not even judge myself. My conscience is clear, but that does not make me innocent. It is the Lord who judges me. Therefore, judge nothing before the appointed time; wait till the Lord comes. He will bring to light what is hidden in darkness and will expose the motives of men's hearts. At that time each will receive his praise from God" (1 Corinthians 4:3-5).

God knows your heart and will someday reveal what happened. You may have misappropriated the promise, but a third choice still remains.

3. *It will be fulfilled at a later time and/or in a way you don't expect*. God promised Abraham that his descendants would be as numerous as the stars in the heavens. He and Sarah were still waiting patiently for its fulfillment after she had passed through menopause and Abraham was about 100 years old. They had even tried to help God fulfill His promise, but all in vain. Abraham had a child by Sarah's handmaiden Hagar, but this wasn't what God had in mind. Old age had come to this family and still there were no children. The natural fulfillment of the promise was not to be. God wanted it fulfilled in a *supernatural* way.

Speaking of this, the writer of Hebrews said, "These were all commended for their faith, *yet none of them received what had been promised*" (Hebrews 11:39). Here were God's heroes of the faith who never lived to see God's promises fulfilled. God fulfilled them in another generation. They did not "abandon ship" and give up. They held tenaciously to the promises and trusted God to fulfill them in His own way.

God has not let you down, and you may not have misclaimed the promise. The Lord may fulfill it in a way and at a time you don't suspect. God's will according to God's timetable is what all of us should be trying to follow.

* * *

It may be helpful to consider the two types of promises found in the Bible:

1. *General Promises.* These are promises given by the Holy Spirit to every believer. When they were penned by the author no individual person or period of time was intended. Rather they are *general,* that is, intended for all people in all generations.

An example of this type of promise is: "If we confess our sins, he is faithful and just and will forgive us our sins and purify us from all unrighteousness" (1 John 1:9). This promise was true for the people to whom John was writing, and it is equally true for you today. There are many such promises throughout the Bible.

2. *Specific Promises.* These are promises given by the Holy Spirit to specific individuals on specific occasions. Like the general promises, specific promises are available to you as the Holy Spirit may lead. The difference is that specific promises must be given expressly to you by the Holy Spirit as they were given to the original recipients. In this sense they are much more subjective than general promises. You can *know* that *all* general promises are given to you, and to everyone else. Specific promises, however, are *available* to you, but don't become yours unless specially given to you by God. Specific promises are most often given for guidance and for blessing.

The Holy Spirit may choose to give you a specific promise to help you determine His will. That is, when He wants to guide you in a particular direction. For example, "Your gates will always stand open, they will never be shut, day or night, so that men may bring you the wealth of the nations—their kings led in triumphal procession'' (Isaiah 60:11).

As you pray over this verse and become increasingly convinced that the Lord wants you to claim it for your life, you may decide to open your home twenty-four hours a day for all whom the Lord sends you. The promise was originally given to the Messiah, but the Spirit of God can give it to you for your ministry.

On their first missionary journey, Paul and Barnabas were opposed by the Jews while they ministered the Word in Antioch of Pisidia. They felt God was calling them to the Gentiles, and to substantiate this leading Paul quoted from Isaiah, ''For this is what the Lord has commanded us: 'I have made you a light for the Gentiles, that you may bring salvation to the ends of the earth' '' (Acts 13:47; see Isaiah 42:6-7). Paul quoted a messianic verse which the Lord had given him for guidance.

Blessing is the other way specific promises are used. The Holy Spirit may not be seeking to guide you, but simply to reveal the blessing He plans for your life. To illustrate this, let us say your church is without a pastor. The last one you had was unsatisfactory, and the leaders of the congregation have been cautious in calling his successor. Months have gone by and you are concerned that the Lord give you the right pastor. As you pray over the situation, the Lord assures you of His promised blessing with the words, ''Then I will give you shepherds after my own heart, who will lead you with knowledge and understanding'' (Jeremiah 3:15).

Because specific promises are subjective, if you have been a Christian for only a short time, it is best to stay with the *general* promises found in the New Testament for the first couple of years. When you think you are ready to claim specific promises, then you should follow certain guidelines:

1. The Spirit of God gives them to individual Christians at particular times in their lives as He chooses.

2. Promises are often conditional and the condition is obedience. You can detect the condition by the presence of the little word *if* in the verse or context.

3. The Holy Spirit of God is sovereign. "But the plans of the Lord stand firm forever, the purposes of his heart through all generations" (Psalm 33:11). He can speak from any passage to any person at any time.

4. Do not prejudge the Lord as to when and how the promise will be fulfilled in your life.

5. God gives His promises to make you more dependent on Him, not independent. Claim them in a spirit of dependence and humility.

6. God's intent is to glorify Himself by giving you promises. Never fail to give Him the glory when the promise is fulfilled.

One further caution is in order before we draw this to a close. When you claim a promise from the Bible, you are determining the will of God in that particular matter. This in turn cuts you off from any further counsel, for who wishes to counsel against the will of God? For example, let us say you are praying and seeking counsel about changing jobs. You claim a promise from the Word that in effect tells you, "It is the will of God to make the change." At that point no further counsel is needed. Now you need to act on what God has said.

In doing this, however, you place full responsibility for the decision on your own shoulders. You have determined God's will by yourself. This is not bad, unless you have misclaimed the promise. The caution comes in making sure you allow for sufficient time and prayer to make the promise a conviction in your soul that this is truly what God wants.

Grammatical Principles of Interpretation

Grammatical principles deal with the very words of the text. How should you understand the words and sentences in the passages under study? What are the ground rules to remember when dealing with the text? These principles answer those questions.

* * *

> ### RULE TEN
>
> **Scripture has only one meaning and should be taken literally.**

In the everyday affairs of life, no serious, conscientious person intends what he says or writes to carry a diversity of meanings. Rather, he desires that the true and obvious sense be understood by his hearers or readers. If you were to say to an audience, "I crossed the ocean from the United States to Europe," you wouldn't want them to interpret your statement to mean that you crossed life's difficult waters into the haven of a new experience. Likewise, no journalist would like to write of the famine and suffering of a country such as India and have his words interpreted to mean that the people of India were experiencing a great intellectual hunger.

As ridiculous as this sounds, much of the ecumenical church does precisely that in their interpretation of the Bible. They call it the use of "connotative words." For example, they don't use *reconciliation* in the biblical sense of a man being reconciled to God. They draw the word from biblical passages, give it their meaning and talk about man's reconciliation with man. *Redemption* is not used in the scriptural sense of man being saved from sin and punishment. Rather, they take this word from a Bible text, give it a different "connotation," and suggest that it has to do with sociological and cultural improvements.

In order to communicate, you must assume (1) that the true intent of speech is to convey thought, and (2) that language is a reliable medium of communication.

The literal interpretation in context, therefore, is the only true interpretation. If you don't take a passage literally, all sorts of fanciful interpretations may result.

When you encounter a passage in which a literal interpretation is indicated from the context and you elect to give it an other-than-literal interpretation, evaluate your motives carefully. As honestly as you can, answer the following questions:

1. *Am I questioning this passage being literal because I do not want to obey it?* For example, Paul said, "Women should remain silent in the churches. They are not allowed to speak, but must be in submission, as the Law says" (1 Corinthians 14:34). Your response is that this was a cultural issue, relevant in its day but not in ours. What led you to that conclusion? A desire *not* to do what the Bible commands or a sincere desire to please God and keep His

commandments? If it is the former, then you are on shaky ground and need to deal with the issue of lordship in your life. If it is the latter, then you are free to pursue your study and see if the rules of interpretation warrant such a conclusion.

2. *Am I interpreting this passage figuratively because it does not fit my preconceived theological bias?* An Old Testament incident gives us an example: ''From there Elisha went up to Bethel. As he was walking along the road, some youths came out of the town and jeered him. 'Go on up, you baldhead!' they said. 'Go on up, you baldhead!' He turned around, looked at them and called down a curse on them in the name of the Lord. Then two bears came out of the woods and mauled forty-two of the youths'' (2 Kings 2:23-24). Your immediate reaction may be that God could never allow such an incident to occur. God is just not like that! Once again you must pause and analyze your motives. Is your response to this passage born out of an embarrassment over what God is reported to have done? If your conclusion is the result of your trying to get God to behave the way you think He should, then again your whole approach to interpretation is wrong. You are God's servant. Your task is to understand who He is and what He expects. The objective of your Bible study is not to confirm *your* ideas of what God is like.

The application of the rules of interpretation must always be founded on a correct motive.

So determine what is the usual and ordinary sense of the word or passage and consider it the correct meaning unless the context demands otherwise.

No statement may be considered to have more than one meaning. No word can mean more than one thing as it is used in a passage. The same word may change meaning within the same sentence as it is used more than once, however. An example of this is, ''God is spirit, and his worshipers must worship in spirit and in truth'' (John 4:24). *Spirit* is used twice in this verse. The first time it refers to the Holy Spirit for it says, ''God is spirit,'' and the Holy Spirit is God. The second use of the word *spirit* can be seen from the context to refer, not to God, but to the totality of the inner person—his essential inner being, his very heart. The word *spirit* changes meaning, but the word cannot mean more than one thing at a time. That is, *spirit* as used the first time can *only* mean God. It can never mean anything else.

When a passage or a word appears to have more than one meaning, choose the clearest interpretation. The most obvious meaning is usually the correct meaning.

This rule is frequently broken. For example, in Jesus' feeding of the 5,000, most people reading the account would accept it as meaning what it says. Yet some interpreters would have us believe that the real meaning of the passage is that Jesus drew out of the crowds a latent spirit of generosity. When they saw the boy share his lunch, they followed his example by pulling their meals out from under their robes.

Before we become overly harsh with those who would misuse the Scripture in this way, we should examine our own practices. The Book of Judges relates the story of Jephthah's vow to God. If God would grant him victory, he would offer in sacrifice the first thing he met when returning home. It was his beloved daughter that he met. Jephthah had vowed, ''I will sacrifice it as a burnt offering'' (Judges 11:31). Then the record states that he ''did to her as he had vowed'' (11:39). You can easily become embarrassed by such stories and conclude that they didn't happen *exactly* the way they were written.

The thought of a man offering his own daughter as a sacrifice to the God of the Scriptures is, to say the least, repugnant. How easy it would be to take the tools of interpretation and draw a different conclusion. As you find yourself yielding to such an urge, remember this important rule of interpretation: *Scripture has only one meaning and should be taken literally.*

RULE ELEVEN

Interpret words in harmony with their meaning in the times of the author.

In the closing days of Jesus' ministry He told several parables about the kingdom of heaven. One of these was the parable of the ten virgins (Matthew 25:1-13). Five were wise because they had sufficient oil for their lamps, and five were foolish because they did not. What was the lamp used for in the ancient wedding feast? What did it look like? These are some questions a student should ask when studying this passage. Here is an example of the need to understand the meaning and use of the word at the time of its writing.

Determining the correct meaning of words found in the Bible is not particularly difficult these days. Many excellent translations are available, and when the meaning of a word is not clear from these, a good Bible dictionary will usually be helpful.

Occasionally the biblical writer will give his own meaning to a particular word. For example, Jesus drove "the changers of money" (John 2:14 KJV) out of the temple. The Jews didn't like this and began arguing with Him. Jesus answered them by saying, "Destroy this temple, and I will raise it again in three days." The Jews then said, "It has taken forty-six years to build this temple, and you are going to raise it in three days?" Jesus, of course, was speaking of the "temple" of His body (John 2:19-21).

John tells us that the temple to which Jesus was referring was His body. Here he gives us the meaning of the word *temple*. Earlier John talked about "changers of money." He did not explain who they were and what they were doing, so you must research the answer to this yourself. By referring to a Bible dictionary or a commentary on the Gospel of John you should find your answer.

Paul interprets the meaning of *me* in his testimony about his own struggles, "I know that nothing good lives in me, that is, in my sinful nature. For I have the desire to do what is good, but I cannot carry it out" (Romans 7:18). *Me* can refer to the will, the intellect, the spiritual or the physical man. Or it can refer to the total person. Paul limits its use here and tells us its exact meaning.

As you study a passage, never skip over words you do not understand. An erroneous impression as to the meaning of a single word can easily obscure the meaning of the sentence and possibly the whole paragraph. Even words you think you understand should be investigated.

An example of this is in Proverbs 29:18. The *King James Version* reads, "Where there is no vision, the people perish." The word *vision* is a poor translation. The marginal reading of the *New American Standard Bible* is more accurate in translating it *revelation*. It refers to the need to be under the ministry of the Word for the purpose of moral restraint. An erroneous impression as to the meaning of the word *vision* obscures the meaning of the statement.

As you study a particular word you should determine four things:

1. *Its use by the writer.* Exciting word studies in English are possible if you care to do a little digging. If the word is central to the thought of the writer throughout the book, it can prove most helpful. For example, the word *sin* is important to the Apostle John. A study of this word as used by him in his first epistle will help you understand the whole letter.

2. *Its relation to its immediate context.* The context will almost always tell you a great deal about the word.

Paul and his companions were ministering in Philippi when he and Silas were arrested, beaten and cast into prison. At midnight while the men were praising God, an earthquake opened the prison doors and it seemed as though all the prisoners had escaped. The jailer was about to commit suicide, but Paul stopped him.

"The jailer called for lights, rushed in and fell trembling before Paul and Silas. He then brought them out and asked, 'Men, what must I do to be saved?' They replied, 'Believe in the Lord Jesus, and you will be saved—you and your household' '' (Acts 16:29-31).

What did the jailer mean when he used the word *saved?* Was it the same as the meaning given it by Paul in verse 31? Since the task of this book is not the interpretation of certain biblical passages, but the presenting of *ground rules* for interpretation, you will have to study the context of the narrative to answer these questions yourself.

3. *Its current use at the time of writing.* This requires a more technical study. Generally a reliable translation gives you the best meaning of the word, since the best available scholarship in the church has been involved in these translations. If you desire to pursue it further, you can use a good commentary.

4. *Its root meaning.* This final way of studying the meaning of a word is generally for the more advanced student of the Bible. Reference works are available that give you the historical background of words. The most comprehensive work is the English translation of the *Theological Dictionary of the New Testament,* edited by Gerhard Kittel and Gerhard Friedrich (Wm. B. Eerdmans Publishing Co., Grand Rapids, Michigan). Other good reference works are *Word Studies in the New Testament* by Marvin R. Vincent (Eerdmans) and *The New International Dictionary of New Testament Theology* edited by Colin Brown (Zondervan). A smaller, one-volume work that is excellent is *An Expository Dictionary of New Testament Words* by W. E. Vine (Fleming H. Revell Co., Old Tappan, New Jersey). Determining the root meaning of a word, however, is not the most important consideration, and you should not be discouraged if you feel it is beyond you.

We have mentioned the existence and blessing of modern translations. Many of them, however, are more paraphrases than accurate translations, and therefore the personal interpretation and bias of the translator is often apparent. As long as the translator or committee are committed to the authority and inspiration of the Scriptures, the danger is not too severe. However, any time the original text is changed for the sake of clarity, a dangerous precedent is being established. An illustration of this is in the *New English Bible's* translation of Genesis 11:1 which begins, "Once upon a time." The Hebrew word is simply *and.* The phrase "once upon a time" is used in fairy tales and suggests to the reader that the story of the building of the Tower of Babel is simply fiction. Whether such a phrase reflects the bias of the translators is a matter of guesswork. Its presence in the Word of God is unfortunate.

The use of modern translations is helpful, but when doing serious study it is best that you stay with one of the reliable translations. These are: The *King James Version* (KJV), the *American Standard Version* (ASV), the *New American Standard Bible* (NASB), the *Revised Standard Version* (RSV), and the *New International Version* (NIV).

When interpreting a word or a passage, your goal is to determine the author's meaning when he wrote it. Try to free yourself of any personal bias when studying a passage. Your objective is to understand the thought of the writer, not what you think he ought to have said.

RULE TWELVE

Interpret a word in relation to its sentence and context.

We have already noted that it is important to study a word in relation to its immediate context (Rule 11). This is so basic and essential in interpreting the Bible that we list it as a separate rule. The best way to explain it will be to have a series of examples from the Bible when this is necessary.

We begin with the word *faith*. It is an important word in the Bible, especially in the New Testament. Yet we find that it has different meanings in different passages. In one letter Paul said, "They only heard the report: 'The man who formerly persecuted us is now preaching the faith he once tried to destroy' " (Galatians 1:23). As you study the context you find that *faith* here means, "the doctrine of the gospel."

When Paul wrote to the Romans he said, "But the man who has doubts is condemned if he eats, because his eating is not from faith; and everything that does not come from faith is sin" (Romans 14:23). Here the context leads you to conclude that *faith* means, "conviction that this is what God wants you to do."

In giving advice to his co-laborer Timothy, Paul said, "But the younger widows refuse, for when they have begun to wax wanton against Christ, they will marry; having damnation, because they have cast off their first faith" (1 Timothy 5:11-12 KJV). Here *faith* means, "a pledge or promise made to the Lord." There is, of course, a relationship between the uses of *faith* in these three passages, but the differences are significant enough to note in order to understand what Paul is saying.

A second example is the use of the word *blood*. Luke recorded the message Paul gave to the Athenians on Mars Hill. In it Paul said, "God that made the world and all things therein, seeing that he is Lord of heaven and earth, dwelleth not in temples made with hands; neither is worshiped with men's hands, as though he needed any thing, seeing he giveth to all life, and breath, and all things; and hath made of one blood all nations of men for to dwell on all the face of the earth, and hath determined the times before appointed, and the bounds of their habitation" (Acts 17:24-26 KJV). Paul has said, "And hath made of one blood all nations." As you study the context it becomes obvious that *blood* means a group of people.

Paul wrote of the salvation we have through Christ: "In him we have redemption through his blood, the forgiveness of sins, in accordance with the riches of God's grace" (Ephesians 1:7). The word *blood* here refers to the atoning death of Christ.

In another Scripture we read, "When everything had been arranged like this, the priests entered regularly into the outer room to carry on their ministry. But only the high priest entered the inner room, and that only once a year, and never without blood, which he offered for himself and for the sins the people committed in ignorance" (Hebrews 9:6-7). *Blood* here refers to that fluid which circulates in the veins and arteries of animals that carries nourishment to the body.

Using a different kind of illustration, we look at Paul's exhortation to the church at Corinth, "Now concerning the things about which you wrote, it is good for a man not to touch a woman" (1 Corinthians 7:1).

Some use this verse to support the idea that a man ought never even to touch a woman in any kind of bodily contact. The context, however, talks about the need to abstain from sexual immorality. In this sense you should not "touch" a woman. It would be erroneous to conclude that a man ought never to touch a woman, like shaking hands with her. In your own study of this passage, you might conclude that in order to maintain sexual purity the Lord would have you avoid physical contact with a member of the opposite sex. It would be wrong, however, to make this application normative for all people.

The ancient manuscripts, from which we make our translations of the Bible, have no punctuation marks. There are no periods, commas, paragraphs, verses, or chapters. These have since been introduced by the translators for clarity and ease of study. When you do your study it is well to remember this. The context will not always be found within the limits of the verse or chapter. You may have to include verses from the chapter before or after.

This study of the context to determine the proper meaning of a word is one of the most basic and important rules of interpretation. You will find yourself referring to it again and again in your study of the Bible.

RULE THIRTEEN

Interpret a passage in harmony with its context.

Each of the writers of the Bible had a particular reason for writing his book(s). As the writer's argument unfolds, there is a logical connection from one section to the next. You must try to find the overall purpose of the book in order to determine the meaning of particular words or passages in the book. These four questions will help:

1. How does the passage relate to the material surrounding it?
2. How does it relate to the rest of the book?
3. How does it relate to the Bible as a whole?
4. How does it relate to the culture and background in which it was written? This fourth question will be handled in a more comprehensive way under *Historical Principles of Interpretation* (Chapter 4), but is important to consider here also.

Answering these four questions becomes especially important when you are trying to interpret a difficult passage. This passage is an example: "No one who lives in him [Christ] keeps on sinning. No one who continues to sin has either seen him or known him. Dear children, do not let anyone lead you astray. He who does what is right is righteous, just as he is righteous. He who does what is sinful is of the devil, because the devil has been sinning from the beginning. The reason the Son of God appeared was to destroy the devil's work. No one who is born of God will continue to sin, because God's seed remains in him; he cannot sin, because he has been born of God. This is how we know who the children of God are and who the children of the devil are: Anyone who does not do what is right is not a child of God; neither is anyone who does not love his brother" (1 John 3:6-10).

When you read this passage by itself, you might conclude that the Christian never sins. Or if he does sin, he cannot be a believer, for "no one who continues to sin has either seen him [Christ] or known him'' (verse 6). If this is the correct interpretation, then only Jesus can ever go to heaven, for He is the only sinless person ever to walk the earth—Christian or non-Christian.

What does this passage mean? How should you interpret it? You must interpret it in the light of its context, and answering these four questions will help you do that.

You will see another example of this in the four Gospels. They have many things in common, not the least of which is that they all give an account of the life, ministry, crucifixion, and resurrection of Jesus Christ. The emphasis of each, however, is different. An understanding of this difference will help you in your study of the parts.

In Matthew we see Jesus as King. He is the fulfillment of all the Old Testament messianic prophecies. Thus you find numerous Old Testament quotations in Matthew.

In Mark Jesus is portrayed as the Servant. The emphasis in this Gospel is on the deeds of Christ. No genealogy is given, for who is interested in the genealogy of a servant?

In Luke Jesus is the Son of Man. Here we note the emphasis given to His humanity. His genealogy is traced back to Adam, the first man.

In John we see Jesus as the Son of God. The Gospel opens by revealing Him as the eternal Word, ''He was with God in the beginning'' (John 1:2).

This is not to suggest that the teachings of one Gospel cannot be seen in the other three. Quite the contrary. The emphasis of each is different. You need to study each Gospel as a whole to catch the panoramic view painted in it. In this way you will see the uniqueness of each, and will be better able to interpret the events and teachings recorded in it.

The importance of this principle cannot be overstated. It is one of the essential rules of interpretation.

RULE FOURTEEN

When an inanimate object is used to describe a living being, the statement may be considered figurative.

The great "I am" passages in John's Gospel illustrate this rule. Jesus said:

"I am the *bread* of life" (John 6:35).

"I am the *light* of the world" (8:12).

"I am the *door* of the sheep" (10:7 KJV).

Jesus is neither *bread* nor a *door* in the literal sense. Because an inanimate object such as *bread* is used to describe the Savior, you can conclude that *bread* must be taken figuratively rather than literally.

Many such examples are found throughout the Bible. The psalmist writes, "The righteous will flourish like a palm tree, they will grow like a cedar of Lebanon" (Psalm 92:12). The righteous person is likened to a palm or cedar tree. Obviously this is figurative language; an inanimate object is used to describe a living being. It is important to have a clear understanding of the thing on which the figure is based or from which it is borrowed. In this example, your study will be enriched by understanding the characteristics of palm and cedar trees and how they grow.

Another example may be drawn from the great prayer of David in which he asks for forgiveness. "Cleanse me with hyssop, and I will be clean; wash me, and I will be whiter than snow" (Psalm 51:7). What is hyssop and how was it used in those days? A study of the ceremonial purification used in Israel will help you have a fuller appreciation for what David was praying.

Periodically you will come across a passage about which there is disagreement in the church as to its figurative or literal interpretation. For an illustration of this, note Jesus' words regarding the Lord's Supper. "While they were eating, Jesus took bread, gave thanks and broke it, and gave it to his disciples, saying, 'Take and eat; this is my body.' Then he took the cup, gave thanks and offered it to them, saying, 'Drink from it, all of you. This is my blood of the covenant, which is poured out for many for the forgiveness of sins' '' (Matthew 26:26-28).

The Apostle Paul, explaining the meaning of the Lord's Table to the Corinthians, virtually uses the same words. ''For I received from the Lord what I also passed on to you: The Lord Jesus, on the night he was betrayed, took bread, and when he had given thanks, he broke it and said, 'This is my body, which is for you; do this in remembrance of me.' In the same way, after supper he took the cup, saying, 'This cup is the new covenant in my blood; do this, whenever you drink it, in remembrance of me.' For whenever you eat this bread and drink this cup, you proclaim the Lord's death until he comes'' (1 Corinthians 11:23-26).

Are the bread and wine in reference to the body and blood of Jesus to be taken figuratively or literally? The church has been and continues to be divided by various interpretations on how the bread and wine are to be understood. You should study the related passages, read what others believe regarding its meaning and why, then form your own convictions. You should, however, allow room for tolerance of the conviction of others regarding their views of the meaning of communion.

* * *

A corollary to this rule is:

When life and action are attributed to inanimate objects, the statement may be considered figurative.

Since this is the same principle viewed another way, one example will bring it into focus.

Micah said, ''Hear, O mountains, the Lord's accusation; listen, you everlasting foundations of the earth. For the Lord has a case against his people; he is lodging a charge against Israel'' (Micah 6:2). When the writer suggests that the mountains ''hear,'' this should be taken figuratively. He is not suggesting that mountains hear and respond as humans do.

The application of this rule and its corollary in your Bible study should come quite naturally. The context more often than not will tell you immediately whether an inanimate object is used to describe an animate being or is ascribed life and action.

RULE FIFTEEN

When an expression is out of character with the thing described, the statement may be considered figurative.

A group of Jews followed Paul throughout Galatia teaching that Gentile Christians had to be circumcised in order to be saved. They became the object of Paul's wrath in his letter to the Philippians. "Watch out for those dogs, those men who do evil, those mutilators of the flesh. For it is we who are the circumcision, we who worship by the Spirit of God, who glory in Christ Jesus, and who put no confidence in the flesh" (Philippians 3:2-3). When Paul warns his readers to beware of the dogs, the context does not warrant concluding that he is talking about those four-legged furry animals used as house pets in the western world. He is referring to those who insisted on imposing on Gentile Christians all the ordinances of the Old Testament. Therefore, *dogs* should be interpreted figuratively.

Jesus was en route to Jerusalem, teaching on the way, when some Pharisees warned Him that King Herod was out to kill Him. To this warning Jesus responded, "Go tell that fox, 'I will drive out demons and heal people today and tomorrow, and on the third day I will reach my goal'" (Luke 13:32). *Fox* refers to Herod; we know from the rest of the Gospels that Herod isn't the name of a fox, but of an evil king, the one who beheaded John the Baptist.

Therefore we can conclude that *fox* must be interpreted in a figurative rather than in a literal way.

Usually the context will tell you whether the statement is figurative or literal, as well as to whom it refers. If you study parallel passages on the subject, they often will help you find the proper interpretation. For example, John the Baptist said concerning Jesus, "Look, the Lamb of God" (John 1:36). This same phrase is used by Isaiah in his great messianic passage: "He was oppressed and afflicted, yet he did not open his mouth; he was led like a lamb to the slaughter, and as a sheep before her shearers is silent, so he did not open his mouth" (Isaiah 53:7). Here the Messiah is referred to as a lamb brought to the slaughter. This and other related passages throughout the Scriptures substantiate the idea that *lamb* is a figurative expression referring to Christ.

At times the same word may be used figuratively, but with different meanings in different places in the Bible. For example, Peter said, "Be self-controlled and alert. Your enemy the devil prowls around like a roaring lion looking for someone to devour" (1 Peter 5:8). Here the context tells you that *lion* refers to Satan.

The Apostle John said, "Then one of the elders said to me, 'Do not weep! See, the Lion of the tribe of Judah, the Root of David, has triumphed. He is able to open the scroll and its seven seals'" (Revelation 5:5). Here, too, *lion* is used, but the context suggests that it refers to Christ. Generally, you can arrive at the correct interpretation from the context.

Quite often figurative language is used to describe God. In His endeavor to communicate with man, He describes Himself with human qualities. The chronicler said, "The eyes of the Lord range throughout the earth to strengthen those whose hearts are fully committed to him. You have done a foolish thing, and from now on you will be at war" (2 Chronicles 16:9). The *eyes of the Lord* is a figurative phrase.

Again, God said to His servant Moses, "Then I will remove my hand and you will see my back; but my face must not be seen"

(Exodus 33:23). The words *hand, back,* and *face* are all to be interpreted figuratively.

> In order for God to speak to us, He must use human figures and imageries in order to convey the divine truth. Nowhere is this so evident as in the Tabernacle in the Old Testament and the parables of the New Testament. In both situations there is a vehicle (the earthly, human) that bears the spiritual truth. Our understanding of the spiritual world is *analogical.* The fact of God's almightiness is spoken in terms of a right arm because among men the right arm is the stronger of the two and with it the most telling blows are delivered. The fact of pre-eminence is spoken of in terms of sitting at God's right hand because in earthly social situations that is the place of honor. Judgment is spoken of in terms of fire because pain from burning is the most intense known in our more general experience, and the gnawing worm is a symbol of that which is slow, steady, remorseless, and painful. Similarly the glories of heaven are in terms of human experience—costly structures of gold, silver, and jewels, no tears, no death, the tree of life, etc. The question as to whether descriptions of hell and heaven are not literal or symbolic is not the point. In either case they are real, e.g., whether it be literal fire, or that spiritual suffering of which fire is the closest symbol.*

In conclusion, note two important things:

1. *A word cannot mean more than one thing at a time.* It cannot have a figurative and literal meaning at the same time. When a word is given a figurative meaning, as has been the case in the illustrations used in this rule, the literal meaning of the word is replaced.

2. *When at all possible a passage should be interpreted literally.* Only if the literal meaning of the word does not fit should it be interpreted figuratively. The literal meaning of a word is always preferred, unless the context makes it impossible.

---

*From *Protestant Biblical Interpretation* by Bernard Ramm. Baker Book House, Grand Rapids, Michigan.

RULE SIXTEEN

The principal parts and figures of a parable represent certain realities. Consider only these principal parts and figures when drawing conclusions.

The ministry of our Lord Jesus was especially rich with parables. He used them to give dynamic and colorful emphasis to spiritual truths. This rule suggests that you should not exceed the intended limits of the parable; don't try to make it say more than it was intended to say. A look at a couple of parables helps us define their limits.

The first is the parable of the sower.

"While a large crowd was gathering and people were coming to Jesus from town after town, he told this parable:

'A farmer went out to sow his seed. As he was scattering the seed, some fell along the path; it was trampled on, and the birds of the air ate it up. Some fell on rock, and when it came up, the plants withered because they had no moisture. Other seed fell among thorns, which grew up with it and choked the plants. Still other seed fell on good soil. It came up and yielded a crop, a hundred times more than was sown.'

"When he said this, he called out, 'He who has ears to hear, let him hear.'

"His disciples asked him what this parable meant. He said, 'The knowledge of the secrets of the kingdom of God has been given to you, but to others I speak in parables, so that, "though seeing, they may not see; though hearing, they may not understand."

" 'This is the meaning of the parable: The seed is the word of God. Those along the path are the ones who hear, and then the devil comes and takes away the word from their hearts, so that they cannot believe and be saved. Those on the rock are the ones who receive the word with joy when they hear it, but they have no root.

They believe for a while, but in the time of testing they fall away.

The seed that fell among thorns stands for those who hear, but as they go on their way they are choked by life's worries, riches and pleasures, and they do not mature. But the seed on good soil stands for those with a noble and good heart, who hear the word, retain it, and by persevering produce a crop'" (Luke 8:4-15).

This is a good parable to study because Jesus gives us the intended interpretation. These verses can be divided into two paragraphs, the parable itself (verses 4-9) and Jesus' interpretation of it (verses 10-15). The principal parts of the parable, as Jesus makes clear in His explanation, are the *seed* and the *types of soil* in which the seed was sown. Though it is often called the parable of the sower, the sower is not the main character. He is incidental to the story.

The purpose of the parable is to illustrate the different types of responses the Word receives when it is proclaimed. As you study the parable, don't extend its purpose beyond the author's intent.

The second parable is Jesus' story of the Good Samaritan.
"A man was going down from Jerusalem to Jericho, when he fell into the hands of robbers. They stripped him of his clothes, beat him and went away, leaving him half dead. A priest happened to be going down the same road, and when he saw the man, he passed by on the other side. So too, a Levite, when he came to the place and saw him, passed by on the other side. But a Samaritan, as he traveled, came where the man was; and when he saw him, he took pity on him. He went to him and bandaged his wounds, pouring on oil and wine. Then he put the man on his own donkey, took him to an inn and took care of him.

''The next day he took out two silver coins and gave them to the innkeeper. 'Look after him,' he said, 'and when I return, I will reimburse you for any extra expense you may have' '' (Luke 10:30-35).

As you interpret this or any other parable, follow this procedure:

1. *Determine the purpose of the parable.* In this example the clue is in the opening question. ''But he wanted to justify himself, so he asked Jesus, 'And who is my neighbor?' '' (verse 29).

2. *Make sure you explain the different parts of the parable in accordance with the main design.* In this parable there was the need, there were those who should have met the need but didn't and there was the meeting of the need from an unexpected source. These parts illustrate the duty of universal kindness and doing good.

3. *Use only the principal parts of the parable in explaining the lesson.* It is when people try to interpret the details that error can easily creep in. Do not make the parable say too much. For example, you may be tempted to suggest that the oil and wine symbolize the Holy Spirit and the blood of Christ (verse 34), the two ingredients necessary for salvation. To do this is to go beyond the intended purpose of the parable.

Determine the main intent of the parable and stay with that. With some parables you will find this easy to do. For example, Jesus asked, ''What shall I compare the kingdom of God to? It is like yeast that a woman took and mixed into a large amount of flour until it worked all through the dough'' (Luke 13:20-21). *Yeast* is a figure which designates a reality, *the kingdom of heaven.* With other parables, you will need to study further before drawing your conclusions.

Each parable has one chief point of comparison. Try to relate this one main point to what the speaker was teaching.

RULE SEVENTEEN

Interpret the words of the prophets in their usual, literal and historical sense, unless the context or manner in which they are fulfilled clearly indicates they have a symbolic meaning. Their fulfillment may be in installments, each fulfillment being a pledge of that which is to follow.

In some ways prophecy is to the Christian what politics is to the secular man, a source of much controversy, heat, and emotion. This rule of interpretation is not meant to bias your conviction on prophecy, but simply to establish a guideline for the formation of your convictions. One of the rules already studied states that "Scripture has only one meaning and should be taken literally" (Rule 10, page 49).

Prophecy should be interpreted literally unless the context or some later reference in Scripture indicates otherwise. An example of where a later reference in Scripture indicates that it cannot be taken literally is the prophecy of Malachi regarding the forerunner of Christ. "See, I will send you the prophet Elijah before that great and dreadful day of the Lord comes. He will turn the hearts of the fathers to their children, and the hearts of the children to their fathers; or else I will come and strike the land with a curse" (Malachi 4:5-6).

Malachi says that God will send "Elijah the prophet." When John the Baptist showed up as the forerunner to Jesus Christ, much confusion was generated, which indicates that the people of that day expected prophecy to be fulfilled literally. Jesus, however, said that this prophecy was to have a figurative rather than a literal fulfillment.

On one occasion Jesus stated, "All the prophets and the Law prophesied until John. And if you are willing to accept it, he is the Elijah who was to come" (Matthew 11:13-14). On another occasion, when His disciples asked Him, "Why then do the teachers of the law say that Elijah must come first?" He answered, "Elijah comes and will restore all things. But I tell you, Elijah has already come, and they did not recognize him, but have done to him everything they wished. In the same way the Son of Man is going to suffer at their hands." Finally the disciples understood that Jesus called John the Baptist Elijah (Matthew 17:10-13). John the Baptist was the fulfillment of Malachi's prophecy.

Such illustrations are the exception rather than the rule in interpreting prophecy. Most prophecies can and should be interpreted literally. There may be times when you can derive two apparent meanings from a prophecy. Give preference to the one that would have been most obvious to the understanding of the original hearers.

There will also be times when a New Testament writer will ascribe to an Old Testament passage a prophetic interpretation when the Old Testament passage does not appear to be prophetic. You will find an example of this in Hosea. Israel had gone away from God and was referred to as the Lord's adulterous wife. God was speaking to Israel when He said, "When Israel was a child, I loved him; and out of Egypt I called my son" (Hosea 11:1). The original hearers could conclude, and rightly so, that this referred to Israel's deliverance from Egypt under Moses. But Matthew quotes this passage and says it is prophetic of Jesus Christ when Mary and Joseph returned with Him to Nazareth. "[He was there in Egypt] until the death of Herod. And so was fulfilled what the Lord had said through the prophet: 'I called my son out of Egypt'" (Matthew 2:15).

We note that the Hosea passage is prophetic because Matthew, writing by inspiration of the Holy Spirit, says it is. In your Bible study you may not take such liberties. Matthew could because he wrote by inspiration of the Spirit, and the Spirit knew the correct interpretation of Hosea since He inspired that also. Matthew, however, does not tell you why he uses the prophecy from Hosea in that way.

Often a prophecy is partially fulfilled in one generation with the remainder fulfilled at another time. At the time when the prophecy is given this is not apparent. It becomes clear when a part is fulfilled and the other is not. It would be much like your looking toward the mountains and seeing but one range. As the prophets looked toward the coming Messiah they saw His two advents as one. As you climb the mountain and descend into the valley on the other side, you see a second range of mountains. You look behind you and see a range; you look in front of you and see another. Christians today are like this in that they stand between the two advents of Christ. Behind us was His first coming; in front of us is His second coming.

We can see in a couple of prophecies that this is what happened. God prophesied through Joel, "And afterward, I will pour out my Spirit on all people. Your sons and daughters will prophesy, your old men will dream dreams, your young men will see visions. Even on my servants, both men and women, I will pour out my Spirit in those days. I will show wonders in the heavens and on the earth, blood and fire and billows of smoke. The sun will be turned to darkness and the moon to blood before the coming of the great and dreadful day of the Lord" (Joel 2:28-32).

Peter quotes these exact words on the day of Pentecost (Acts 2:15-21). When the Spirit descended on the church Peter said, "This is what was spoken by the prophet Joel" (Acts 2:16). Indeed the Spirit was poured out upon them. But when did the sun turn into darkness and the moon into blood, "before the coming of the great and dreadful day of the Lord"? This portion of Joel's prophecy refers to the Second Advent and will be fulfilled in the future. From Joel's perspective the two advents appeared as one.

We can observe the same thing in Isaiah's prophecy concerning the Messiah. "The Spirit of the Sovereign Lord is on me, because the Lord has anointed me to preach good news to the poor. He has sent me to bind up the broken-hearted, to proclaim freedom for the captives and release for the prisoners, to proclaim the year of the

Lord's favor and the day of vengeance of our God, to comfort all who mourn'' (Isaiah 61:1-2).

Jesus was in His hometown of Nazareth when He went into the synagogue to worship on the Sabbath. ''The scroll of the prophet Isaiah was handed to him. Unrolling it, he found the place where it is written: 'The Spirit of the Lord is on me; therefore he has anointed me to preach good news to the poor. He has sent me to proclaim freedom for the prisoners and recovery of sight for the blind, to release the oppressed, to proclaim the year of the Lord's favor.' Then he rolled up the scroll, gave it back to the attendant and sat down. The eyes of everyone in the synagogue were fastened on him, and he said to them, 'Today this scripture is fulfilled in your hearing' '' (Luke 4:17-21).

As you compare the Nazareth declaration with the prophecy in Isaiah, you note that Jesus stopped reading in the middle of the sentence (Isaiah 61:2). He left out the words, ''and the day of vengeance of our God, to comfort all who mourn.'' This part of the prophecy refers to Christ's second coming. Isaiah combined the prophecy regarding the two advents. From his vantage point they appeared as one.

Recognizing this will help you in your Bible study as well as encourage your heart. For the fulfillment of the first installment is a guarantee of its total fulfillment; just as the Holy Spirit is a down payment or guarantee of your inheritance in Christ. Be encouraged. He came the first time as promised. He will come the second time also, as prophesied!

4 Historical Principles of Interpretation

The historical principles deal with the historical setting of the text. To whom and by whom was the book written? Why was it written and what role did the historical setting play in shaping the message of the book? What are the customs and surroundings of the people? These are the kinds of questions you try to answer when considering the historical aspect of your study.

* * *

RULE EIGHTEEN

Since Scripture originated in a historical context, it can be understood only in the light of biblical history.

As you begin your study of a passage, imagine yourself to be a reporter searching for all the facts. Bombard the text with questions such as:

- To whom was the letter (book) written?
- What was the background of the writer?
- What was the experience or occasion that gave rise to the message?
- Who are the main characters in the book?

Your objective is to place yourself into the setting at the time the book was written and feel with the people involved. What were their concerns? How did God view their situation? Feel the pulse, if you can, of the author as he expresses himself.

A brief background on the Book of Galatians may help bring the importance of this rule into focus.

The New Testament church as God gave it birth was Jewish. The chosen people of the Old Testament were Hebrews and it was from among the Jews that Jesus chose His disciples. On the day of Pentecost (Acts 2) the non-Jews or Gentiles who were converted were all proselytes of or converts to Judaism. These early followers of Jesus *assumed* that the way to Christ was through the Jewish religion. This was *not* so much a matter of conviction; it was simply the way it happened.

Then Cornelius came to Christ without being circumcised into Judaism (Acts 10), and this caused no small stir among the believers. But this soon quieted down and the subject did not present itself again till the ministry of Paul got under way. Paul, the great scholar of Judaism who was tutored by the famous Rabbi Gamaliel, was God's chosen instrument to refine the doctrine of how Gentiles could become Christians.

While on his first missionary journey, Paul began including Gentile converts in the fellowship of the church without first bringing them through the laws of Judaism. To many Jewish Christians this was unacceptable. The more legalistic of them began to follow Paul's ministry through the Roman province of Galatia (modern-day Turkey), preaching that these Gentile Christians had to be circumcised into the Jewish religion.

Paul was furious. But what could he do? The only Scriptures the church had at that time were the books of the Old Testament, and the Old Testament was what these Judaizers were preaching to the Galatians. When he returned to Jerusalem, Paul attended a council of the church leaders and posed the question to them (Acts 15). Does a Gentile need to become a Jew first before becoming a

Christian? How is a man justified before God? "By faith apart from the works of the law" was Paul's contention.

The leadership at the Jerusalem council agreed with Paul. This marked a major change in the direction of the church. Before this Christianity was not considered to be a separate religion. It was viewed as the natural evolution of Judaism—its fulfillment. From this point on Christianity began to be seen as distinct from the Jewish religion.

How was Paul going to share this news with the Galatians? How could he undo the damage caused by the Judaizers? Paul turned to Old Testament law and proved from the law that the law cannot save. Throughout the letter to the Galatians numerous quotes come from the Old Testament law. The Old Testament law, not Paul, preaches that a man is justified by faith apart from the law.

Understanding the historical background helps in understanding and interpreting the Book of Galatians. This type of study will pay rich dividends and you will find it indispensable in the interpretation of any passage you study.

RULE NINETEEN

Though God's revelation in the Scriptures is progressive, both Old and New Testaments are essential parts of this revelation and form a unit.

It is not uncommon to hear a person say, "The God of the Old Testament is different from the God of the New Testament. In the Old Testament He seems so harsh and judgmental, while in the New Testament He is more loving and gracious." Though this is a commonly held belief, it is not based on fact and, if held, will lead you astray in your interpretation of the Bible. For example, Jesus talked more about hell and the judgment of God than did anyone else in the Bible.

The Old Testament sets the stage for the correct interpretation of the New

Testament. You would have difficulty understanding what the New Testament is talking about if you were unfamiliar with the Old Testament account of such events as the creation and the fall of man. Jesus assumes that His listeners are familiar with the account of how the Israelites were bitten by serpents for their murmurings and delivered by looking to a serpent of brass placed on a pole (Numbers 21). Referring to this event Jesus said, "As Moses lifted up the snake in the desert, so the Son of Man must be lifted up" (John 3:14).

In another sense, the New Testament is a commentary on the Old Testament—how God revealed Himself and how His plan is progressive. The further you read, the more you know about Him and what He plans to do. The New Testament explains the purpose of much that happened in the Old Testament.

The whole Book of Hebrews is an example of this. Unless you are familiar with the Old Testament tabernacle, priesthood, and sacrificial systems, you will have difficulty following the argument in the book. This letter explains the purpose and significance of the Old Testament forms of worship.

People were saved in Old Testament times the same way they are saved in the New. Justification before God has always been by faith. In the Old Testament people were saved by faith in Christ (the Messiah) who *was* to come. In the New Testament we are saved by faith in Christ who *has* come. Jesus said, "I am the way—and the truth and the life. No one comes to the Father except through me" (John 14:6). This is as true for the Old Testament as for the New Testament.

The means and content of this salvation become progressively clearer as Old Testament history unfolds. The prophet Isaiah understood more than Adam, but not as much as we do today. But it is clear that there is a unity between the Old and New Testaments on how people are saved.

The unity of the Scriptures can also be seen in the frequent quotations of the Old Testament in the New. Matthew, showing that Jesus is the fulfillment of the Old Testament prophecies, quotes about 70 times from the Old Testament.

From the fall of Adam to the consummation of history all people need Christ as their Redeemer. All believers are born anew by the Holy Spirit. All receive the same inheritance of heaven. God used different methods to communicate these truths. For example, in the Old Testament one of the signs and seals of the covenant relationship was the observance of the Passover and the eating of the paschal lamb; in the New Testament it is the celebration of the Lord's Supper. But the truths themselves are applicable in both testaments.

God does progressively reveal Himself as history unfolds. But this does not mean that God's standards become progressively higher or that God changes along the way. Rather, it is our understanding of God and His revelation that is progressive. God never changes.

Certain practices in the Old Testament were cancelled by the New Testament, but that is only because they found their fulfillment in Christ. An example of this is the offering of animal sacrifices. When Christ, the perfect sacrifice, offered Himself, there was no longer a need to offer animals. These animal sacrifices were a preview of what God planned to do through Jesus Christ. But the Scriptures make it quite clear that animal sacrifices could not save, "for it is impossible for the blood of bulls and goats to take away sins" (Hebrews 10:4).

God's character in the Old Testament did not change by some process of moral evolution. His perfect holiness is an unchanging, uncompromising part of His nature. For example, Jesus was interrogated on the subject of divorce (Matthew 19). Some argued in its favor on the basis of the law of divorce in the Mosaic code. "Why then," they asked, "did Moses command that a man give his wife a certificate of divorce and send her away?" (verse 7; see Deuteronomy 24:1-4).

Jesus replied, "Because of your hardness of heart, Moses permitted you to divorce your wives; but from the beginning it has not been this way" (verse 8). Jesus said that the laws against divorce were temporarily set aside in the Old Testament because of the moral callousness of the people, not because of any change in the character of God or His moral requirements.

God's revelation of Himself is progressive as you read through the Bible, but His character is unchanging. God's great plan of redemption is the same in both testaments. As you study the Bible you can consider them two parts of the same book, not two separate books.

RULE TWENTY

Historical facts or events become symbols of spiritual truths only if the Scriptures so designate them.

Webster defines *symbol* as "something that stands for or suggests something else by reason or relationship, association, convention, or accidental resemblance; especially a visible sign of something invisible." Though there are differences between the words *symbol, type, allegory, simile,* and *metaphor,* they are closely enough related to combine them here. This rule applies to all of them since they are often used as visible signs of something invisible.

An example of the Bible's use of a historical event as a symbol of a spiritual truth is Paul's statement:

"For I do not want you to be ignorant of the fact, brothers, that our forefathers were all under the cloud and that they all passed through the sea. They were all baptized into Moses in the cloud and in the sea. They all ate the same spiritual food and drank the same spiritual drink; for they drank from the spiritual rock that accompanied them, and that rock was Christ" (1 Corinthians 10:1-4).

Israel's passing through the Red Sea (Exodus 14:22) symbolized their baptism. The rock from which Israel drank (Numbers 20:11) was a type of Christ. In a number of places the writer borrows from a historical event to represent a spiritual truth.

To carry this further than Paul does would be to detract from the literal meaning of the passage. To say that the Red Sea symbolizes the atoning blood of Christ, which offers a safe way to the heavenly Canaan, is an improper interpretation of the Corinthian passage.

This same rule is also applied to allegorizing. As Paul develops his theme in the Book of Galatians, that justification is through faith in Jesus Christ apart from the law, he uses an allegory to drive home his point. Not only does he allegorize Sarah and Hagar (who both bore Abraham children), he tells us he is doing so. "For it is written that Abraham had two sons, one by the slave woman and the other by the free woman. His son by the slave woman was born in the ordinary way; but his son by the free woman was born as the result of a promise. These things may be taken figuratively, for the women represent two covenants. One covenant is from Mount Sinai and bears children who are to be slaves: This is Hagar" (Galatians 4:22-24).

Paul made these interpretations of the Old Testament under the inspiration of the Holy Spirit. He did so occasionally and for specific reasons. But for you to make a habit of allegorizing historical facts is to detract from the literal interpretation of the Bible and to change its intended meaning. The objective of Bible study is to understand the intended meaning of the author, not to pour into his words your own content.

A negative example often helps, especially when a passage has been used to symbolize something that it should not have.

A common Scripture so used is the Book of Philemon. Paul is writing to his good friend Philemon on behalf of a runaway slave, Onesimus. Onesimus, the slave of Philemon, had robbed his master and fled to Rome. There, through Paul, he became a Christian and Paul was sending him back to his master in Colosse with this letter. Paul's plea to his friend is that he forgive Onesimus and restore him as "a dear brother." "If he has done you any wrong or owes you anything, charge it to me," was Paul's request (verses 16, 18). It is a beautiful example of Christian love, forgiveness, and brotherhood.

For no apparent reason many allegorize this book, equating Philemon with God, Onesimus with mankind and Paul with Christ. Christ (Paul) intercedes with the Father (Philemon) on behalf of the converted runaway (Onesimus). Paul does not make this analogy here or in any other passage. Neither should you.

This kind of allegorizing is different from making application. For example, we can say that what Paul was asking of Philemon on behalf of Onesimus is what Christ did for us. We should in the same way forgive those who have wronged us. Our application is drawn from the historical event or fact without changing the intended meaning of the fact.

5 Theological Principles of Interpretation

Theology is the study of God and His relation to the world. The source book for this study is the Bible. Theology seeks to draw conclusions on various broad and important topics in the Bible. What is God like? What is the nature of man? What is a proper doctrine of salvation? These are the kinds of subjects with which theology deals. Theological principles are those broad rules that deal with the formation of doctrine. For example, how can we tell if a doctrine is truly biblical? One of our theological principles will seek to answer this.

* * *

RULE TWENTY-ONE

You must understand the Bible grammatically before you can understand it theologically.

Another way to state this rule is to say, "You must understand what the passage says before you can expect to understand what it means." An example of this may be seen in this Pauline statement:

"But the gift is not like the trespass. For if the many died by the trespass of the one man, how much more did God's grace and the gift that came by the grace of the one man, Jesus Christ, overflow to the many! Again, the gift of God is not like the result of the one man's sin: The judgment followed one sin and brought condemnation, but the gift followed many trespasses and brought justification. For if, by the trespass of the one man, death reigned through that one man, how much more will those who receive God's abundant provision of grace and of the gift of righteousness reign in life through the one man, Jesus Christ.

"Consequently, just as the result of one trespass was condemnation for all men, so also the result of one act of righteousness was justification that brings life for all men. For just as through the disobedience of the one man the many were made sinners, so also through the obedience of the one man the many will be made righteous.

"The law was added so that the trespass might increase. But where sin increased, grace increased all the more, so that, just as sin reigned in death, so also grace might reign through righteousness to bring eternal life through Jesus Christ our Lord" (Romans 5:15-21).

You must study this passage carefully to understand what Paul is saying. He is comparing Christ with Adam. Just as you are considered to be unrighteous because of the sin of Adam, so you are considered to be righteous because of what Jesus Christ did. The sin of Adam was imputed to you, even though you did nothing to deserve it; so also the righteousness of Christ was imputed to you, even though you did nothing to deserve it. This, in part, is what the passage says.

From this we can draw certain conclusions. For example, we see that imputation does not affect your moral character, but your legal standing. When you were considered righteous because of the work of Christ your moral character was not changed; you did not become morally righteous and perfect, only legally righteous and perfect in the sight of God. This is why some non-Christians are more righteous in their behavior than Christians.

Another example is this statement: ''If we deliberately keep on sinning after we have received the knowledge of the truth, no sacrifice for sins is left'' (Hebrews 10:26). Many use this verse to teach that it is possible for a Christian to lose his salvation. A study of this verse in its context leads you to an entirely different conclusion. This passage speaks specifically to Jews who believed in animal sacrifices in anticipation of the coming Messiah, not realizing that He had already come.

The writer to the Hebrews sets forth the fact of Jesus' sacrifice. This statement says that once these Jews understood the reason for Jesus' death and deliberately ignored it, if they returned to their sacrifices there would be no future sacrifice provided by God.

You can see how such a problem can be alleviated by using sound grammatical principles (Rules 10-17). You must understand what a passage says before you draw any doctrinal conclusions from it.

RULE TWENTY-TWO

A doctrine cannot be considered biblical unless it sums up and includes all that the Scriptures say about it.

It is immediately apparent that this is an important procedure in Bible study, just as it is in all of life. Solomon warned, "He who answers before listening—that is his folly and his shame" (Proverbs 18:13). It is foolish to come to a conclusion before hearing all of the arguments. So also, it is a mistake to come to conclusions regarding a certain doctrine before studying all the Bible says on the subject.

For example, there are numerous passages in the New Testament which tell you that you are not under the law. "For we maintain that a man is justified by faith apart from observing the law" (Romans 3:28). "But if you are led by the Spirit, you are not under law" (Galatians 5:18). When reading such statements, can you conclude that the grace of God frees you from any obligation to live a disciplined, holy life?

Not at all. Such a conclusion would be countered by statements such as: "What shall we say, then? Shall we go on sinning so that grace may increase? By no means! We died to sin; how can we live in it any longer? Or don't you know that all of us who were baptized into Christ Jesus were baptized into his death? We were therefore buried with him through baptism into death in order that, just as Christ was raised from the dead through the glory of the Father, we too may live a new life" (Romans 6:1-4).

This is where a topical type of Bible study proves useful. You take a theme, idea, or teaching and study all the passages on the subject. Three kinds of parallel studies are:

1. *Word Parallels.* You may, for example, decide to study the life of Balaam. The main passage regarding him is found in Numbers 22–24. He was one of God's prophets who allowed

himself to be enticed by an invitation from the king of Moab to curse Israel. What conclusions can you draw from his life? A study of what the New Testament writers say of Balaam will help in your evaluation. Peter tells us that he ''loved the wages of wickedness'' (2 Peter 2:15). Jude tells us that he was greedy for profit (Jude 11). John further informs us that he counseled the king of Moab to ''entice the Israelites to sin by eating food sacrificed to idols and by committing sexual immorality'' (Revelation 2:14).

2. *Idea Parallels*. An idea parallel differs from a word parallel in that you can't cross-reference the word, as you can with Balaam. The idea is more encompassing than any one word. An example might be the whole question of authority. The chief priests and elders asked Jesus, ''By what authority are you doing these things? . . . And who gave you this authority?'' (Matthew 21:23). You would want to study not only this passage in Matthew 21, but many other passages in the Scriptures on the subject. Moses records man's first rebellion against authority (Genesis 3); Scripture also shows God dealing severely with those who rejected the authority of one of His servants (Numbers 16).

3. *Doctrinal Parallels*. This would include topical studies on the great doctrines of the Bible such as the attributes of God, the nature of man, redemption, justification, and sanctification.

In this type of study you gather all the pieces of information together and draw a conclusion. It is much like putting the pieces of a puzzle together. This is called *inductive reasoning,* that process of reasoning from all the parts to the whole. If you were going to study the doctrine of the church inductively, for instance, you would find all the passages on the subject, study each one, and then put them all together to form your conclusions.

In Rule 24 we will consider a principle dealing with *deductive reasoning,* but we need to look briefly at deductive reasoning here. This is the method that approaches the study by looking at the whole and coming to conclusions regarding the smaller pieces, again, like a jigsaw puzzle. From the whole puzzle you can conclude certain things about the individual pieces. Deductive reasoning is that process of reasoning from the general to the particular. An example of deductive reasoning is:

• *First Premise*—If we ask according to His will, God hears us (1 John 5:14-15).

• *Second Premise*—Sanctification is according to God's will (1 Thessalonians 4:3).

• *Conclusion*—When we pray for our sanctification, God hears us.

The reason we are discussing deductive reasoning here is the need to relate it to your inductive study. As a general rule, the first premise in your *deductive* study can be made only after *inductive* study has brought you to the understanding of what the premise is and means. Other examples of *deductive* study may be seen in Rule 24.

Inductive Bible study is extremely important in developing your convictions. As you study the parts you are able to get an increasingly clearer picture of the whole. If you are not involved in an inductive study, you should be. For if your convictions regarding the doctrines of the Bible have been formed by what others have told you, rather than by your own personal investigation of the Scriptures, will they stand during times of testing? You cannot count on remaining faithful during times of adversity on the basis of hearsay. You must dig into the Scriptures for yourself and get your own convictions.

Unfortunately, as is so often the case, what is important requires hard work. This is true in the formation of vital convictions. Careful and thorough Bible study is required. No shortcut exists. Your doctrinal studies form the backbone of your spiritual convictions, and these in turn can be arrived at only by studying all that the Bible says on a given subject.

RULE TWENTY-THREE

When two doctrines taught in the Bible appear to be contradictory, accept both as scriptural in the confident belief that they resolve themselves into a higher unity.

A number of seeming contradictions or paradoxes exist in the Scriptures. "Seeming" because they really are not. They appear contradictory because the finite mind of man cannot comprehend the infinite mind of God.

Some familiar paradoxes to the human mind are:

1. *The Trinity.* We do not serve three Gods, but one, yet *each* Person in the Godhead is fully and completely God, not just one-third God. In essence we must conclude that one plus one plus one equals one. No human illustration can adequately explain this theological mystery. It is utterly beyond our comprehension.

2. *The dual nature of Christ.* Jesus Christ is all God and all Man. He is not half God and half man; yet He is not two persons but one. Again one plus one equals one.

3. *The origin and existence of evil.* Logically the human mind deduces that one of two things must be true. Either God created evil, or it is coeternal with Him. The Bible leads us to believe that neither is true. It is a mystery.

4. *The sovereign election of God and the responsibility of man.* Paul states that God has chosen the believer in His sovereign counsel before the foundation of the world (Ephesians 1:4). Yet Peter says, "The Lord is not slow in keeping his promise, as some understand slowness. He is patient with you, not wanting anyone to perish, but everyone to come to repentance" (2 Peter 3:9). All through the Scriptures there is a well-meant offer of the gospel to

all men. Man is viewed as a responsible moral agent who is held accountable by God, and "everyone who calls on the name of the Lord will be saved" (Romans 10:13). There is no way that our minds can reconcile these two difficult and seemingly opposite truths.

Of all the difficulties none causes as much emotional controversy as the last one. Possibly this is because the first three strike us as rather academic, while the fourth touches our moral sensibilities. It has to do with man's eternal destiny.

When the Bible leaves two "conflicting" doctrines unreconciled, so must you. Living in tension is not pleasant, but you must take care not to lose biblical balance in seeking to relieve the tension. Do not wrench the Scriptures apart in an attempt to force two "conflicting" doctrines into compromise.

You can make application of such "conflicting" doctrines by preaching the right doctrine to the right person. For example, as a Christian you preach to yourself that God chose you; you did not choose Him. If the choice had been yours, you would have voted *against* Him. All you are and have is a gift of God's grace. This should fill you with humility and meekness.

But you can boldly proclaim to the non-Christian that God loves him. For Jesus Himself said, "God so loved the *world* that he gave his one and only Son" (John 3:16).

Our allegiance is not first and primarily to a system of theology, but to the Scripture. When you interpret the Bible, don't allow human logic to make it say any more or less than it in fact says. To the degree that the Scriptures speak with clarity, you may speak with clarity. When the Scriptures are silent, you must remain silent. Where the Bible teaches two "conflicting" doctrines, you must follow its example and hold to both, keeping each in perfect balance with the other.

RULE TWENTY-FOUR

A teaching merely implied in Scripture may be considered biblical when a comparison of related passages supports it.

The Jewish religious community in Jesus' time was split into various groups: Herodians, Essenes, Zealots, Sadducees, and Pharisees. These last two groups were divided over certain doctrinal issues, notably the resurrection of the dead. The Pharisees believed it; the Sadducees denied it.

On one occasion Jesus found Himself in an argument with the Sadducees on this question of the afterlife. Did the Old Testament really teach it? Listen to Jesus' line of reasoning, "Now about the dead rising—have you not read in the book of Moses, in the account of the bush, how God said to him, 'I am the God of Abraham, the God of Isaac, and the God of Jacob'? He is not the God of the dead, but of the living. You are badly mistaken!" (Mark 12:26-27).

The Lord said that the resurrection could be proved from the Old Testament (Exodus 3:15), where God identified Himself as the God of Abraham, Isaac, and Jacob. Since God is the God of the living, these three men must be alive or resurrected. This is deductive reasoning, and could be charted in the following form:

- *First Premise*—God is the God of the living.
- *Second Premise*—God is the God of Abraham, Isaac, and Jacob.
- *Conclusion*—Abraham, Isaac, and Jacob are among the living.

The doctrine of the resurrection is *implied* in the Old Testament, reasoned Christ. It is not expressly stated in the Old Testament that there is a resurrection of the dead, but when you compare related passages on the subject you deduce that such is true.

Another example is the question of admitting women to the Lord's Table. We conclude that they should be admitted to communion, but not on the basis of any specific command or example in the Bible, since none is given. We assume that they should be admitted on the basis of the *implied* teachings of the New Testament. In this example, the deductive process is as follows:

When Paul wrote to the Corinthian church, it is obvious that women were members of the church. "My brothers, some from Chloe's household have informed me that there are quarrels among you" (1 Corinthians 1:11). "The churches in the province of Asia send you greetings. Aquila and Priscilla greet you warmly in the Lord, and so does the church that meets at their house" (1 Corinthians 16:19). Both Chloe and Priscilla were women. Paul also instructed the church on how to conduct itself at the Lord's Supper (1 Corinthians 11). Therefore we infer from these passages of Scripture that women partook of communion.

- *First Premise*—The Corinthian church received instruction on communion.
- *Second Premise*—Women were part of the church at Corinth.
- *Conclusion*—Women may partake in communion.

You must be certain the deductions you make are truly implied in the Scriptures from which you derive them, and that you have investigated and compared related passages on the subject. It is easy to misuse the principle and arrive at unbiblical conclusions. This is frequently done with passages that give us examples from the life of Christ.

Mark says of Jesus, "Very early in the morning, while it was dark, Jesus got up, left the house and went off to a solitary place, where he prayed" (Mark 1:35). From this we are likely to deduce that a faithful Christian should have his quiet time in the early morning.

- *First Premise*—The believer is to be Christlike.
- *Second Premise*—Christ had early morning devotions.
- *Conclusion*—The believer should have early morning devotions.

Yet, you will remember that under Rule 5, *Biblical examples are authoritative only when supported by a command,* we discussed this, using this very example. Using the reasoning spelled out here you can properly conclude that you *may* have early morning devotions, but not that you *must* have them. This passage supports the validity of the quiet time in the morning, but not its necessity.

You cannot violate one principle of interpretation in order to substantiate another. Your Bible study must take all the principles into account if you are to make a proper interpretation.

Believing something to be true because of an implied teaching in the Bible is not only valid, but also necessary (Jesus' argument for the resurrection from the Old Testament, for example). Like Rule 23, however, such reasoning requires careful study, and this is hard work; but the fruit of such labor is rewarding and well worth the effort.

Do not be afraid to use deductive reasoning in your Bible study. In everyday life, you do it all the time. Suppose you are working for a data processing firm and you have been on this job for some time. Today, as you are going to work, you find yourself returning to that job even though your employer did not specifically ask you to come in this day. You are doing it because you reason:

- *First Premise*—Your employer wants you as an employee.
- *Second Premise*—Your employer has had you on this particular job for some time.
- *Conclusion*—Your employer wants you on that job today.

Think back on the number of times you have *deduced* something to be true on the basis of certain facts; or how someone *implied* something to be true even though he did not specifically say so.

This process is valid in your Bible study as well, providing you abide carefully by Rule 24.

11 How to Study the Bible

Bible Study Is for Everyone

The scene before our eyes is the vast expanse of wilderness between Jerusalem and the Jordan River. In preparation for His public ministry, Jesus had fasted 40 days and nights in this barren expanse, alone, hungry, and weary. Satan now confronts Him with three insidious temptations. Three times our Lord wards off his suggestions by quoting from the Book of Deuteronomy.

Recognizing that the Bible is authoritative for the Savior, Satan tries his hand at quoting Scripture too. He selects the psalmist's statement, "For he will command his angels concerning you to guard you in all your ways; they will lift you up in their hands, so that you will not strike your foot against a stone" (Psalm 91:11-12; see Matthew 4:6).

As you compare Satan's words with the text in Psalm 91, it is interesting to note that he does not *misquote* the psalmist. Rather, he misuses the passage by misrepresenting the intent of the writer.

The tactics of our enemy have not changed through the centuries. Since Satan misrepresented the Scriptures to Jesus Christ, the believer today can be assured of the same thing happening to him. But how does the devil do this? From what quarter are we to expect his attacks?

Ways in Which the Bible May Be Misused

Five ways immediately come to mind, and others could be added to this illustrative list.

1. *The Scriptures may be misused when you are ignorant about what the Bible says on a given subject.*

The ordination of avowed, practicing homosexuals into the gospel ministry is an example. Some would have the church believe that the loving, accepting spirit of our Lord Jesus precludes their being barred from ordination. Nowhere did Jesus say they shouldn't be ordained, so the church should ordain them as clergy in good and regular standing. Yet the Old Testament expressly forbids acts of homosexuality (see Leviticus 18:22), and Paul states that homosexual behavior contributes to God's wrath on mankind (see Romans 1:26-27). Ignorance about what the Bible teaches is an open door to the attack of the enemy.

2. *The Scriptures may be misused when you take a verse out of context.*

On the night of His betrayal Jesus said to His disciples, "Until now you have not asked for anything in my name. Ask and you will receive, and your joy will be complete" (John 16:24). Some have taken this to be a carte blanche promise from God. He will grant whatever you ask. That same night, however, a short while after making this statement, Jesus prayed in the Garden of Gethsemane, "Take this cup from me. Yet not what I will, but what you will" (Mark 14:36). Promises in the Bible must be blended with the total context of the scriptural teaching on prayer (see 1 John 5:14-15).

3. *The Scriptures may be misused when you read into a passage and have it say what it doesn't say.*

Toward the end of His ministry, Jesus said, "And these signs will accompany those who believe: In my name they will drive out demons; they will speak in new tongues; they will pick up snakes with their hands; and when they drink deadly poison, it will not hurt them at all" (Mark 16:17-18). Some have taken this descriptive passage to be a command to do all of the things mentioned, reading into it a mandate to do all of these when all Jesus is doing is describing what is going to happen in situations in the early church when certain people had the gift of miracles.

4. *The Scriptures may be misused when you give undue emphasis to less important things.*

Did Judas, the betrayer of our Lord, participate with Jesus and the other disciples in the Last Supper? The evidence is inconclusive, yet some allow themselves to become greatly exercised over an issue such as this, even to the point of contributing toward disunity in the church.

5. *The Scriptures may be misused whenever you use the Bible to try to get God to do what you want, rather than what God wants done.*

Let us use the example of a woman who is in love with a man and wants very much to marry him. Jesus said, "Again, I tell you that if two of you on earth agree about anything you ask for, it will be done for you by my Father in heaven" (Matthew 18:19). Taking this promise to a girlfriend, she asks the woman to join her in claiming this promise in order to "get" the man. This is an obvious misuse of the Scriptures.

The Need for Bible Study Methods

Not every misuse of the Bible can be attributed to an attack from Satan, even in the illustrations just mentioned. It becomes immediately apparent, however, that you must learn to use the Scriptures carefully. Christians must not only become familiar with the rules of interpretation (see pages 17-91), but they must apply these rules to a life-long habit of Bible study. The objective of this second section of the book is to introduce you to Bible study methods. Much good material is already available on this subject, but the intent here is to take some methods of Bible study and make them simple enough for the average layman to incorporate into his Christian life.

Unlike the subject of interpretation, Bible study methods have a great deal of flexibility and require some creativity. These methods are not "rules" of Bible study per se, but are guidelines which, if followed, will enhance the study of the Scriptures. We will explore these methods in the following chapters. No matter how masterful or conscientious a student of the Bible you may be, you must maintain vigilance in staying fresh and creative. So experiment with the various methods. Pick and choose from what is offered and add your own ideas. Make the method yours. Remember, there is a difference between doing Bible study which can be drab and perfunctory on the one hand, and studying the Bible which is exciting and life-changing on the other.

Principles of Bible Study

When I was a fledgling seminarian, a layman sat down with me and introduced me to five principles of Bible study. He helped me realize the importance of going to the Scriptures as my primary source, rather than gleaning spiritual truths from studies other men have made. By principles, he meant that they ought to be included in our Bible study, irrespective of the method we might employ.

1. *You must do original investigation.* An incident in the early church illustrates the importance of the believer getting alone with an open Bible and depending on the Holy Spirit to be his teacher: "Now the Bereans were of more noble character than the Thessalonians, for they received the message with great eagerness and examined the Scriptures every day to see if what Paul said was

true'' (Acts 17:11). The Bereans listened attentively to what Paul and Silas had to say, but elected to check it out with the original source.

It is important that conviction be formed on what the Bible teaches, rather than depending on creeds, commentaries, or even sermons. The latter may cause you to turn to the Word as did the Bereans, but during times of testing it is the authority of the infallible Word personally examined that stands.

Two types of resource materials may be used in Bible study. Biblical encylopedias, dictionaries, and concordances are one type, and should be the constant companion of the student. Commentaries and other expository works are the second type. But these should only be used *after* the principle of original investigation has been applied.

Referring to a good commentary after the study is completed is helpful, particularly if you teach your material to others or lead a Bible study group. It becomes a way of checking your ideas and conclusions with others. If you find yourself in disagreement with the commentator, especially on significant issues, you should then take a fresh look at *your* conclusions.

Original investigation is a necessary and important principle to incorporate into your methodology. There is something fresh and exciting about a truth taught by the Holy Spirit during your personal time in the Word of God.

2. *You must have written reproduction.* Have you ever had the experience of thinking a profound thought, but because you did not write it down you forgot it? If so, you probably discerned that the harder you tried to remember the thought, the more elusive it became. Such a frustrating experience illustrates the importance of incorporating written reproduction into your Bible study methods.

Dawson Trotman, founder of The Navigators, often would say, ''Thoughts disentangle themselves as they pass from the mind through the lips and over the finger tips.'' Writing down your thoughts and drawing them together is one of the key differences between Bible reading and Bible study. A rich reservoir of scriptural knowledge can be stored for future use when written reproduction is employed.

3. *Your study must be consistent and systematic*. Two concepts make up this third principle. Bible study should be consistent. This is implied in the words *every day* in Acts 17:11. The Bereans didn't study the Scriptures one day, then wait a week to do it again. Their approach was *consistent*.

The other concept embedded in this principle is that Bible study must be systematic. A chapter here, a topic there, a passage another time are not the best approaches to studying the Bible. Map out a program of Bible study that will systematically unfold for you a balanced understanding of God's whole Word. Such an approach is suggested in the Appendix.

4. *Your study must be "pass-on-able."* This conglomerate may sound strange, but it does communicate an important concept. It is found in Paul's statement to Timothy: ''And the things you have heard me say in the presence of many witnesses entrust to reliable men who will also be qualified to teach others'' (2 Timothy 2:2). It is God's intention that we not only grow and mature in our walk with Him, but also help others to maximize their potential for Jesus Christ.

Each believer is to view himself as a link between two generations. We are to *pass on* to others what we have had the privilege of learning. If we apply this only to the content of our study we encourage people to become dependent on us for ''intake.'' The biblical concept of the priesthood of the believer means that all Christians have both the right and the responsibility of feeding personally on the Word of God. Our Bible study methodology must include the element of pass-on-able-ness to facilitate this great ideal.

5. *You must apply what you study to your life.* So important is this principle that we find it incorporated in the rules of interpretation as well as the methodology about to be studied. A cursory reading of almost any portion of the Bible reveals how important application is from God's perspective. He *expects* His Word to be taken seriously. James tersely said, "Do not merely listen to the Word, and so deceive yourselves. Do what it says" (James 1:22).

Basic Steps of Bible Study

In Chapter One you were introduced to four essential parts that form the foundation for all Bible study—observation, interpretation, correlation, application. Because these parts *are* basic to your study of the Word, irrespective of the kind of study in which you engage (such as, analytical, synthetic, or topical), it is necessary to look at each individually and at some length.

Each of the four parts will be presented in such a way as to move from the simple to the more advanced. As you apply these parts to your study of the Scriptures, you will be encouraged to select your own level of difficulty, adding various techniques as you become increasingly proficient.

The format of the following chapters will introduce you to five methods of Bible study, beginning with a basic study and moving toward more advanced steps. Each of them will use the four parts of Bible study—observation, interpretation, correlation, application. You have enough information given you in Chapter One, however, to do all these studies, but when you begin to feel at home with them, go on to Chapters 13–16 for information on more advanced elements of the four parts.

As you begin to do these studies, follow the *Basic* sections only (to the **STOP** sign). Do *not* go on to the *Advanced* sections till you have mastered the basic approach. The methods do not have to be done in the presented order; you may try your hand on them in any order. The basic studies are on the following pages:

After you are comfortable with any of the *Basic* approaches, you have the choice of going in two directions: (1) Proceed to do the *Advanced* steps of the method you have chosen, or (2) go more in depth in your *Basic* study by turning to the suggestions in Chapters 13–16.

If you are just beginning a program of Bible study, you may want to consider starting with a question-and-answer method to get the "feel" of it. An outstanding series on this method is *Studies in Christian Living,* published by The Navigators. (This set and individual booklets are available from your local Christian bookstore or from Customer Services, NavPress, P.O. Box 20, Colorado Springs, Colorado 80901.) This series consists of nine booklets, progressing from the simple to the more difficult. Not only do they introduce you to two Bible study methods, they also expose you to all the major teachings of the Bible.

Doing these is not a prerequisite to the material in Chapters 7–11, but if you find the following difficult, you may want to start with the question-and-answer approach.

7 The Verse Analysis Method of Bible Study

VERSE ANALYSIS

The study of a single verse in the Bible with reference to its immediate context.

The verse analysis method of Bible study is the simplest "on-your-own" study. But don't let its simplicity fool you. It is an extremely profitable and rewarding method of Bible study, and a wonderful place to begin. Many have found the fruits of such a study so rewarding that they find themselves continually returning to it for the feeding of their souls.

Bible study is only one method of scriptural intake. You should also be engaged in a Bible reading program. Ideally, it is from this reading program that you select the verse to be studied. In the margin of your Bible, or on a separate sheet of paper if you prefer, note possible verses to be studied.

When you are ready to begin your study, select from these possibilities the one on which you want to concentrate.

You may also want to consider the possibility of memorizing the verse. This combination of Bible study and Scripture memory is unbeatable in sealing the verse to your own heart.

To draw attention to the four basic parts of Bible study, you will note next to each step a letter indicating the part you are doing.

(O) OBSERVATION
 (I) INTERPRETATION
(C) CORRELATION
(A) APPLICATION

As you become more proficient in your use of the *Verse Analysis* method, you may want to refer to the chapters dealing with these parts for additional things to look for.

Basic Verse Analysis

For the purpose of illustration, 1 Thessalonians 5:17 will be used in walking through this procedure: "Pray without ceasing" (KJV).

(O) *Step One*—Select the context of the verse and note the boundaries. If it is difficult to determine this, refer to a modern translation such as the *New International Version,* which notes the paragraph divisions. If the context is a rather long paragraph, you may either want to try breaking it down further or choose another verse to study.

The context of 1 Thessalonians 5:17 are the verses immediately preceding and following: "Rejoice evermore" (verse 16 KJV) and "In everything give thanks, for this is the will of God in Christ Jesus concerning you" (verse 18 KJV).

(O) *Step Two*—Note any observations and/or possible applications. Also look for any problems, stating specifically what the problem is. You will want to add to this section of your study constantly as you proceed through the other steps.

1 THESSALONIANS 5:16-18

(O) ● There are three commands—*rejoice, pray, give thanks.*

(O) ● These commands all have modifiers—*evermore, without ceasing, in everything.*

(O) ● The clause "This is the will of God in Christ Jesus concerning you" seems to apply to all three verses.

(O) ● You can interchange the modifiers with one another without changing the meaning of the verses: *"Rejoice evermore, pray evermore, give thanks evermore,"* and so on with the other modifiers.

(A) ● Giving thanks (verse 18) is not one of my strong points. I tend to grumble about everything.

(A) ● I rejoice (sometimes), but not "always."

(I) ● The modifiers all have the idea of being perpetual, that is, there is never a time when they shouldn't be done.

(I) ● Can verse 17 be taken literally? Is it possible to pray unceasingly? Or is Paul simply talking about an attitude here?

(I) *Step Three*—Briefly rewrite each of the verses in your own words. Try to express the kernel of thought or main idea the writer is communicating.

1 THESSALONIANS 5:16-18

● Verse 16—Never stop rejoicing
● Verse 17—Never stop praying   God's will for you
● Verse 18—Never stop giving thanks

(C) *Step Four*—Cross reference each of the verses with another similar idea in the Bible. The best commentary on Scripture is Scripture. Look for verses that will help explain, illustrate, or in some way clarify the idea.

1 Thessalonians 5:16-18

- Verse 16—Philippians 4:4
- Verse 17—Ephesians 6:18
- Verse 18—Romans 1:21; Ephesians 5:20

(A) *Step Five*—Choose from the possible applications the one God would have you work on, stating the problem, an example of the problem, the solution, and the specific thing God would have you do to apply the solution.

1 Thessalonians 5:16-18

- Verse 18—I am convicted by the fact I am unthankful. Just yesterday I realized that I had not thanked my wife for all the hard work she does in cooking, keeping house, taking care of the children, and many other things.
- I purpose before God to begin checking this ingratitude and replacing it with verbal expressions of thanksgiving.
- I will apologize to the Lord and to my wife and ask their forgiveness.
- Each day this week I will ask God's help in this during my morning devotions and seek to implement it during the day.
- I will talk this over with children and ask them to call to my attention any failures to express gratitude to my wife.

Do not go on to the Advanced section until you have mastered these five basic steps.

Advanced Verse Analysis

After you have done the above study for a period of time, feel comfortable with it, and want to proceed further, you may try the next four steps. Bible study should not become burdensome or complicated. Don't add these steps prematurely to your study. Nor should you feel "less spiritual" if you never add them. Methodology must always be your servant, never your master.

(I) *Step Six*—Select the pivotal idea in the passage. This is the word or phrase around which the thought moves. Ask yourself, *Is the principal thrust of this passage to exhort to some action or to teach a doctrine?* If action, then concentrate on the verbs. The key is likely to be found there. If doctrine, concentrate on the nouns.

1 THESSALONIANS 5:16-18

- Verse 17—The pivotal word is *pray*. It is the *means* of appropriating God's grace enabling you to *rejoice. Giving thanks* is the *method* of prayer.

(I) *Step Seven*—In one sentence write the distilled essence or theme of the passage. Tie the verses together into one "big idea."

1 THESSALONIANS 5:16-18

- God's will for the believer is that in prayer he thanks God for all circumstances so as to rejoice perpetually.

(C) *Step Eight*—Chart the passage, seeking to draw the parts into a whole and relating them to one another. The various methods of chart making are outlined in Chapter 15, pages 189-214.

1 THESSALONIANS 5:16-18

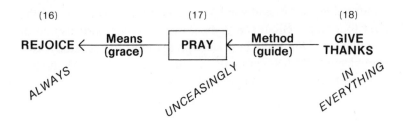

(I) *Step Nine*—Choose a title for the passage

1 THESSALONIANS 5:16-18

- *Title:* "The Will of God in Christ Jesus for Me"

8 The Analytical Method of Bible Study

ANALYTICAL STUDY
The careful examination of a chapter or passage in the Bible.

To analyze something is to study the object in detail, being careful to note even the most minute aspects. This is the objective of analytical Bible study. Here we seek to examine a passage carefully and thoroughly. The purpose is to understand what the writer had in mind when he wrote to his audience.

In many ways the analytical method can be contrasted with the synthetic method of Bible study, which is the topic of Chapter 9. In the synthetic study you will look at the larger picture, as through a telescope. Here in the analytical method you study the parts as through a microscope. Using the illustration of a library, in the synthetic approach you are looking at the composition of the library, while in the analytic approach you are studying the contents of each book.

Analytical Bible study is the "meat and potatoes" of your study of Scripture. As the years progress, you will, in all probability, lean on it as the mainstay of your Bible study program. It is basic for a thorough knowledge of the Word, allowing the student opportunity to interface with why the writer said what he did the way he did. Again, the objective is to reconstruct as clearly as possible the original thinking of the writer.

Question-and-answer Bible studies are a form of the analytical method, as is the verse analysis method presented in Chapter 7. The study on which we are about to embark will launch you into studying a whole passage on your own.

As in verse analysis, a letter indicating the part you are doing is noted next to each of the steps to draw attention to the four basic parts of Bible study.

(O) OBSERVATION
(I) INTERPRETATION
(C) CORRELATION
(A) APPLICATION

As you become increasingly proficient in your use of the analytical method, you may want to refer to the individual chapters dealing with these parts for additional help.

Basic Analytical Study

For the purpose of illustration, 1 Peter 2 will be the chapter analyzed in walking through the procedure.

(O) *Step One*—Read through the passage carefully. Take a sheet of paper and mark OBSERVATIONS on the top. This will be used throughout the study. Include on this sheet:

1. Observations—Note any and every detail you notice. Bombard the passage with questions such as who? what? where? when? why? and how? Note nouns, verbs, and other key words.

2. Problems—Write out what you don't understand about the passage. Don't say, "I don't understand verse 4." Rather, elaborate on what it is you don't understand. Some of your questions will resolve themselves as you continue your study. Others will be resolved only by referring to an outside source such as your pastor or a commentary. Some of your questions may never be answered.

3. Cross-references—Using the book *Treasury of Scripture Knowledge* or the marginal references in your Bible, cross reference the word, quote, or idea with a similar text elsewhere in the Bible. This will help in your understanding of the passage.

4. Possible applications—You will observe several of these in the course of your study. Note them on this sheet with an (A) in the margin. At the conclusion of your study you will return to these possible applications and select the one on which the Holy Spirit will have you focus.

The following is a sample list of observations taken from 1 Peter 2. They are all listed in this illustration, but you should remember that the list is *not* completed in *Step One* before going on to *Step Two*. You will be adding to the observations throughout the entire study. Don't be concerned that the observations be sequential. If you are half way through the chapter, and have a fresh thought about verse 1, note it right there. Don't worry about trying to squeeze it in at the top of the page.

1 PETER 2 — OBSERVATIONS

(**I**) • Verse 1—To follow this advice is to become alienated from the world, for this is how the world acts. Not to follow it is to be alienated from God.

(**C**) • Verse 3—Psalm 34:8.

(**O**) • Verses 1, 11—Sanctification is one of the emphases of 1 Peter. It must be in three directions: (1) toward God

(1:13)—hope, have faith, appropriate God's grace; (2) toward others (2:1)—related to the last six of the Ten Commandments; and (3) toward self (2:11)—these are sins that primarily hurt the person committing them.

(O) • Verses 4-8—Three quotes from the Old Testament are used to explain the use of *stone* in reference to Jesus Christ (Isaiah 28:16; Psalm 118:22; Isaiah 8:14).

(O) • Verses 9-10—Who are we? We are a . . .

—*Chosen people*—the word *chosen* is also used in 1:2. We have been chosen to obedience (1:2), and we have been chosen for service (2:9). Sanctification is our goal and obedience is the process.

—*Royal priesthood*—in verse 5 it was a *holy* priesthood; here it is a *royal* one, with the imagery probably taken from Melchizedek, the king-priest in the Old Testament (Genesis 14).

—*Holy nation*—collectively we are the people of God and form a unique nation, one that has holiness as its hallmark. Our goal is not to be like the world, but to be like Jesus Christ.

—*Peculiar people* (KJV)—we are a people especially suited for God to possess. The older expression *peculiar* means "to bring about or obtain for oneself." God has obtained us to be a people for Himself.

(A)   —We were not always those four things, so we should praise God because He has changed us:

1. From darkness to light—from sin to glorious salvation.

2. From being no people to God's people—from insignificance to purpose and meaning.

3. From receiving no mercy to having mercy in abundance—we do not have to face judgment for our sins.

(A) • Verse 13—"every authority instituted among men." We must obey every law that does not violate God's laws whether the government is favorable or hostile, and we do it for the Lord's sake (see Acts 4:19; 5:25).

(O) • Verses 15, 19-20—the *two reasons* given in this section for submission and serving are: (1) demonstrate to the world that God's call is to a life of good and not evil; and (2) God is pleased with such conduct, since it is a reflection of the character of Jesus Christ (see verses 21-25).

(O) • Verses 13, 15—the two commands given in this section are *submit* and *serve*.

(O) • Verses 13-14, 18—the two groups to whom we are to submit and whom we are to serve are the *government* and *employers*.

(O) • Verses 13-20—possible outline for this section: "Submissive Servants—the Example of the Believer to the World."
   1. Divine Despotism (verse 16)—proper perspective
   2. Demonstration (verse 17)—proper attitude
   3. Divine Directive (verses 13, 18)—proper life style
   4. Two Groups (verses 13-14, 18)
   5. Two reasons (verses 15, 19-20)

(O) • Verse 25—we are very much like straying sheep, but Christ has brought us back to Himself. He is shown to be:

   —*the Shepherd*—one of the oldest descriptions of God in the Bible (see Isaiah 40:11). He took care of His sheep—His people—even better than a shepherd in Judea took care of his sheep—the animals.

   —*the Overseer*—this word means one who presides over, guards and protects. This is what Christ is to His people (see Matthew 28:20).

The observations in this section will vary in length, depending on how much time you are able to give to the study. Don't become discouraged if you don't "observe" much the first few times you do the study. With practice your observations will increase in number and in depth.

(I) *Step Two*—Take another sheet of paper and divide it in two parts, leaving ⅔ of the space on the left and ⅓ on the right. On the *far* left, write numerals down the page according to the number of verses in the chapter (25 for 1 Peter 2). On the left ⅔ of the sheet, verse by verse, state the key thought, that is, the main teaching, subject, or thought the writer is communicating in the content of the verse. (At times you may have difficulty verbalizing the key thoughts of certain verses, such as 1 Peter 2:1.)

On the remaining ⅓ of the sheet, try to combine the key thoughts of the verses into summary key thoughts. Try to feel the flow of the writer's argument. As you combine verses, it will become apparent where the paragraph divisions in the chapter are located.

It is important to note the flow of ideas in a passage—the relationship of the verses to one another. Sometimes the writer makes a general statement, then explains it with examples (see 2 Timothy 3:1-5). At other times he may list a series of ideas and then summarize with a general statement (see James 2:14-17). Or he may give a command, warning, or advice and back them up with reasons, purposes, or proofs. Try to determine what it is the writer is doing in the presentation of his material. Note the way he moves from one idea to the next. See Figure 1 for an example of 1 Peter 2.

(I) *Step Three*—Take a third sheet of paper and place it next to the sheet used in *Step Two*. You are now ready to begin tying the chapter together.

Looking at your *Summary of Key Thoughts* (right ⅓ of the

1 PETER 2 — KEY THOUGHTS AND SUMMARIES

VERSE	KEY THOUGHTS	SUMMARY OF KEY THOUGHTS
1.	Put away your sin	
2.	Like babies, crave the milk of the Word	1-3 Put away sin; take in the Word
3.	Assuming you have tasted God's goodness	
4.	Come to God's rejected Stone — Christ	
5.	You are a living stone to God's honor	
6.	The O.T. tells us to believe in The Cornerstone	4-8 Like a cornerstone, Christ is built on or rejected
7.	Unbelievers have rejected God's Cornerstone	
8.	In their disobedience they stumble over Him	
9.	God has chosen you to proclaim Christ	9-10 You once rejected Christ, but are now His
10.	Once you were outside of Christ, but are now His	
11.	Stay away from fleshly desires	11-12 Holiness is the best testimony
12.	Let the uncommitted glorify God for your deeds	
13.	Obey the laws of the land	
14.	The law punishes the bad and praises the good	
15.	Let your good silence those who condemn the Gospel	13-17 Believers as free men are to obey the law and love others
16.	Use your freedom for good, not evil	
17.	Love others — fear God	
18.	Servants are to obey their masters	
19.	God will reward the servant whose master is cruel	18-20 Servants are to submit — even to cruel masters
20.	You are specially rewarded when suffering for good	
21.	In this you are to follow Christ's example	
22.	Christ was sinless	
23.	When punished for good, He did not retaliate	21-25 Christ's response to rejection is our example
24.	His suffering was punishment for our sins	
25.	Like wandering sheep you have returned to Him	

Figure 1

previous sheet), divide the chapter into its paragraphs. These are easily determined by the natural breaks in the writer's flow of thought.

Write a key thought for each paragraph. The key thought for each paragraph will be a combining of all summary statements on that paragraph. Likewise, the key thought of the chapter will be a summary of the key thought of your paragraphs. What you are doing here is funneling the passage in such a way as to distill its essential meaning (see Figure 3). The key thought for the paragraph is the distilled essence of that paragraph in one sentence and the key thought of the chapter is the distilled essence of the chapter in one sentence. Make each of these sentences as brief as possible without sacrificing the main truth.

You can take each paragraph and put subpoints under it. This is especially helpful if the paragraph(s) tend to be long. This is an optional part of *Step Three*.

1 PETER 2 — OUTLINE

I. Verses 1-10—By studying the Word of God, the Christian is to reflect the character of Christ, who is God's cornerstone, rejected by men.
   A. Strip off the world; drink in the Word (verses 1-3)
   B. Stone of stumbling or salvation (verses 4-8)
   C. Showcase of contrast (verses 9-10)

II. Verses 11-25—Christ set an example for the Christians on how to respond to a world that does not know Him.
   A. Sanctified living is the best testimony (verses 11-12)
   B. Submission—the Christian's example to the world (verses 13-20)
   C. Submission—Christ's example to the believer (verses 21-25)

(A) *Step Four*—Choose from the possible applications the one God would have you work on: stating the problem, an example of the problem, the solution, and the specific things God would have you do to apply the solution.

1 PETER 2—APPLICATION

- Verse 13—"Submit yourselves for the Lord's sake to every authority instituted among men." The Lord has spoken to me regarding my habitually exceeding the speed laws. When I drive my auto, I almost always go faster than the speed limit.

    For example, the other day I was on my way downtown and caught myself with one eye looking ahead and the other behind, to see if I would be caught speeding by the police. I know the Lord would have me slow down.
- More often than not, I speed because I am late for an appointment. This happens because of laziness on my part. To make application, I will:
    1. Ask the Lord's forgiveness.
    2. Declare myself on this issue to my family and friends, and ask that they remind me when I exceed the law.
    3. Leave early for every appointment, so I won't have the pressure of disobeying the "authority instituted among men."

STOP

Do not go on to the Advanced section until you have mastered these four basic steps.

Advanced Analytical Study

If, after doing these four steps for a period of time, you want to add to your study, you can do two things. One is to read Chapters 13–16 and implement those parts of observation, interpretation, correlation, and application that apply to these four steps of the basic study. The other is to add further steps to your study. Be bold and imaginative in this. Try new things. Methods are designed to help you, not enslave you. Put aside what doesn't work for you and add what does. Remember, the objective of Bible study is to determine the meaning of the writer at the time he wrote it, and apply this truth to your life. Everything else is methodology to help you in this quest.

The following are five other steps you can add if and when you feel ready.

(I) *Step Five*—Select the pivotal idea in the passage. This is the word or phrase around which the thought of the passage moves. Ask yourself, *Is the flow of the passage in the direction of exhortation to action, or teaching doctrine?* If action, then concentrate on the verbs. The pivotal idea is likely to be found there. If the flow of the passage is on teaching doctrine, then concentrate on the nouns.

On a separate sheet of paper make two columns. List the key verbs in one and the key nouns in the other, verse by verse. Study these lists and determine if the thrust of the chapter is in the direction of action or doctrine.

Look for the appropriate verb or noun (or perhaps phrase) that is amplified in some respect in each paragraph of the passage. This is the pivotal idea. If there is more than one that qualifies, then choose the best one.

After studying these parallel bits in Figure 2, you can see that 1 Peter 2 is an exhortation to action. From the important verbs listed, the key ones are circled. Peter's exhortation is to follow His (Christ's) example (verse 21). ''Follow His Example,'' then, is the pivotal idea of the passage.

(I) *Step Six*—The *key thought of the passage* is the essence of the passage in one sentence. The key thought of each paragraph is how the writer develops that passage. This was determined in *Step Three*. By now you have discovered that finding the *pivotal idea (Step Five)* is helpful in determining the *key thought of the pas-*

1 PETER 2 – PIVOTAL IDEA

VERSE VERBS	NOUNS
1. rid (yourselves)	malice, deceit, hypocrisy, jealousy, slander
2. crave, grow	babies, milk (Word, S.C.), salvation
3. taste	Lord, good
4. come	Stone
5. are being built, offering, acceptable	stones, house, priesthood, sacrifices
6. trusts	cornerstone
7. believe, rejected	stone, builders, capstone
8. causes, makes, stumble	stone, rock, message
9. you are, declare	people, priesthood, nation, darkness, light
10. were not, (now) are	people, God, mercy
11. abstain	(sinful) desires, soul
12. live, see	(good) lives, deeds
13. submit	authority, king
14.	governors
15.	
16.	
17. show . . . respect, love, fear	
18. submit (yourselves)	slaves, masters
19. bears up	commendable, God
20. suffer	
21. (you) were called, follow	Christ, example
22.	
23.	
24.	
25.	Shepherd, Overseer

Figure 2

sage, which we will elaborate on here in *Step Six.* This whole process is illustrated in Figure 3.

THE FLOW OF THE WRITER'S ARGUMENT

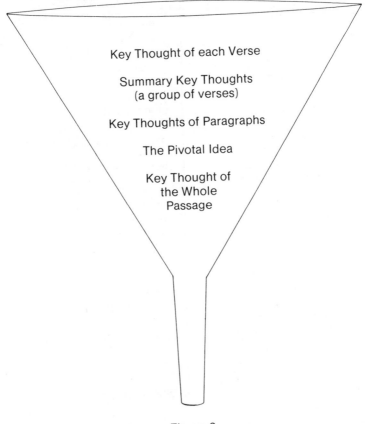

Key Thought of each Verse

Summary Key Thoughts
(a group of verses)

Key Thoughts of Paragraphs

The Pivotal Idea

Key Thought of
the Whole
Passage

Figure 3

The *key thought of the passage* should then be developed as the eminent truth of the passage. In doing so, state the *key thought of the passage* at the beginning and end of your eminent truth. The development of the key thought of the passage is the articulation of the writer's message and follows the flow of the passage (see Figure 3 above). You can have only *one* key thought to the passage. Each person doing a study may state it in his own words, but it should become immediately apparent in a comparison of key thoughts written by various people that they are all studying the same passage. A correct application of the above six steps should lead everyone to the same conclusion. This is illustrated in Figure 4.

I Peter 2 — Key Thought of the Passage

The Christian is called on to follow the example of Christ into a life of submission and suffering at the hands of a hostile world.

EMINENT TRUTH

The Christian is called on to follow the example of Christ and live a life of submission and suffering at the hands of a hostile world.

The holiness of Jesus Christ was such a contrast to a sinful world that men either had to conform to Him or destroy Him. Peter uses the illustration of a cornerstone. The cornerstone properly laid insured that the building would be straight and solid. Prior to Christ all "buildings" (lives of people) were crooked. The contrast wasn't seen till Christ the perfect "building" appeared. He was rejected and crucified (verses 4-8).

Christ's suffering and rejection was *caused* by the sinfulness of man and *resulted* in the salvation of man. His death on the cross (verse 24) paid the penalty for sin and brought a solution to man's problem.

All of this was possible, however, because Christ understood His role and was submissive to it (verses 22-23). So we also must understand our roles and be submissive to them. Our holiness (verses 1, 9, 11, and others), like Christ's, evokes a negative reaction from a sinful world (verse 20). Thus sinful men persecute us just as they did Him. Our response must be to *serve* and *submit*. This example will aid in God's plan of redemption (verses 12, 15). In short, we are to *follow His example* (verse 21).

The Christian is called on to follow the example of Christ into a life of submission and suffering at the hands of a hostile world.

Figure 4

AN EXAMPLE TO FOLLOW

	SANCTIFIED TO GROW	CHRIST REJECTED	WHO WE ARE	SANCTIFIED TO BEHOLD	HOW WE OUGHT TO LIVE	CHRIST'S RESPONSE TO REJECTION
	2:1-3	2:4-8	2:9-10	2:11-12	2:13-20	2:21-25
	GROW	COME	DECLARE	ABSTAIN	SUBMIT	FOLLOW
	DESTINY			**DUTY**		
	— — BE SUBMISSIVE — — —					
	FOR YOUR OWN SAKE			FOR THE SAKE OF THE WORLD		
	CHRIST THE STONE			CHRIST THE SHEPHERD		

Figure 5

(I) *Step Seven*—Write a title for each paragraph and then for the whole chapter (or passage). The purpose of a title is *identification*. It is a tool to help you recall the passage and its contents. Here is where you can show your creativity, and may want to use something catchy.

---

1 PETER 2—TITLE

"An Example to Follow"

Figure 6

(C) *Step Eight*—Charting a passage is a way of relating the part to the whole and comparing the various parts with one another. Read Chapter 15, pages 189-214, which explains the various techniques for charting, and chart the passage you have just studied. See Figure 5 for an example.

(O) *Step Nine*—For the truly ambitious, a ninth and final step you may incorporate is to memorize the passage. Though such a task is hard work, it pays rich rewards. As you review the passage, fresh observations and insights will come to mind which you can add to your *Observation* section *(Step One)*. The following suggestions are for your consideration.

1. Memorize from only one translation. Use the one from which you are studying.

2. Place the verses on cards—one verse per card—putting the verse on one side and the reference on the other. (Blank cards specifically designed for this may be obtained from your local Christian bookstore, or by writing Customer Services, NavPress, P.O. Box 20, Colorado Springs, Colorado 80901; 1,000 cards for $2.50.)

3. Review, *Review*, REVIEW. Few things are as frustrating as memorizing a portion of Scripture and then forgetting it. Review is hard work, but keep current in it.

4. Memorize the passage *before* you begin your study. This will help you in every step you employ. It will tie the passage into a unit and give you the ability to have the whole in mind as you study it verse by verse.

Do not allow the methodology to overwhelm you. For example, in the five advanced steps, choose only those with which you feel comfortable. In time you may want to design a new step and use it. There is nothing sacred about methodology. Its value lies in its ability to help you become a more proficient student of the Word of God.

The Synthetic Method of Bible Study

The synthetic method of Bible study approaches each book of the Bible as a unit and seeks to understand its meaning as a whole. The objective is to get a broad, panoramic view of the book. It does not concern itself with details but the overall scope of the book.

In the analytical method you looked at the text through a microscope. In the synthetic method you look at it through a telescope. What did the writer, moved by the Holy Spirit, have in mind as he wrote? What is the key thought or big idea in the book? How does he make his point? These are the kinds of questions that are germaine to the synthetic method.

This method is probably the most difficult of all the Bible study methods, but can also prove to be the most rewarding.

As in every method of Bible study, you will incorporate four basic parts:

(O) OBSERVATION
(I) INTERPRETATION
(C) CORRELATION
(A) APPLICATION

Next to each step in the study you will note one of the above four letters. These are meant to alert you to the part employed in that step. Further information on how to approach each of these four parts may be found in Chapters 13–16.

Basic Synthetic Study

For the purpose of illustration, the Book of Romans will be synthesized in walking through the procedure.

(O) *Step One*—Read through the book carefully. Take a sheet of paper and mark *Observations* on the top. This will be used throughout the entire study. Include on this sheet:

1. Observations—Note the key thoughts or main arguments that flow through the book. List the important words. Note such things as places, events, and important names. List things you may want to study later.

2. Problems—When you are unable to follow the thinking of the writer, note when this occurs and exactly what it is you don't understand.

3. Cross-references—Note any important events or quotes the writer uses from other parts of the Bible. For example, Romans 10:18-21 refers to a series of quotes from the Old Testament (Psalm 19:4; Deuteronomy 32:21; Isaiah 65:1-2). An understanding of the context of each of those quotes will help you discover the flow of Paul's argument in the Book of Romans.

4. Possible Applications—Several of these will come to your attention as you read and reread the book. Note these for use later in your study.

Figure 6 is a sample list of observations taken from the Book of Romans. They are all listed on one page, but it should be remembered that the *Observations* are *not* completed in *Step One* before going on to *Step Two*. Rather, use this sheet throughout the entire study and add to it as you go along.

(I) *Step Two*—Read the book through a second time, involving yourself in a process of intensive exploration. Your objective is to unravel the writer's argument. As you read, list under your *Observations* the key thoughts or major themes of the book. Try to put them in your own words. Don't let the chapter and verse divisions destroy the unity of the book, for these divisions were not there when the writer penned his book originally. Be sure to do this reading in one sitting.

(The illustration of *Step Two* is included in *Step One* in Figure 6.)

(I) *Step Three*—Read the book carefully a third time. Ask the Holy Spirit to enable you to approach it with a fresh mind. With a pen in your hand complete your reading in one sitting.

As you read this time, look for the main theme or big idea the writer is communicating. This is the key thought of the book—the organizing principle that gives the book its unity.

Is there any particular place in the book where the key thought is mentioned? Does any one verse or passage state the idea more succinctly than any other? If so, note this.

As you compare this key thought with the themes listed in *Step Two*, the unity should become apparent. Write the key thought out in your own words.

ROMANS — Observations

VERSE   OBSERVATIONS

1:18   Paul begins his epistle by establishing the fact of man's sin. He deals first with the world at large (1:18-32), then the moralist (2:1-16), and finally the Jew (2:17 – 3:9).

3:21-26   Here we see the solution to our problem—the death of Christ—a beautiful, logical flow in Paul's teaching.

2:7   What does this mean? Is Paul here saying that a person can *work* his way to heaven?

3:1   The Jews had a tremendous advantage. So do I as a man
(**A**)   born in a Christian heritage. I should list all the advantages I have that much of the world does not.

4:1   Why does Paul talk about Abraham after Christ?

5:12-21   What is the gist of Paul's argument in this passage? What is he seeking to communicate?

6:1-4   A beautiful picture of our identification with Christ in His death, burial, and resurrection.

Whole   Outline:
            1. Man's need (1:1 – 3:20)
            2. God's solution (3:21 – 5:21)
            3. Implication for Christians (6:1 – 8:39)
            4. Implication for Jews (9:1 – 11:36)
            5. Application (12:1 – 16:27)

9:3   Paul wished himself "accursed" from Christ for his kinsmen.
(**A**)   Do I have that kind of love for people?—a real challenge!

11:1-32   Paul seems to indicate that there will be a future for Israel? Is this for the nation or just certain individuals? What does "ALL" in verse 26 mean?

12:19   "Avenge not yourself"—I find that I tend to be vindictive
(**A**)   toward people who I feel have wronged me.

13:2   Does this passage imply that the thirteen colonies were wrong in declaring their independence from Britain in 1776?

14:1-23   This is a passage on Christian liberties. It has far-reaching implication for the church today. Note the question and answer method Paul uses in communicating.

Figure 7

ROMANS—KEY THOUGHT

Romans 1:16-17—*The just shall live by faith.*

(C) *Step Four*—Read the entire book a fourth time. Approach your reading as though you are exploring the book for the very first time. Don't "breeze" through it. Again, do this reading at one sitting. Be sure and set aside adequate time so as not to be interrupted.

This time through, develop a broad outline of the book. Be more interested in the flow of the writer's thinking than the chapter divisions. Resist the temptation to use the outline found in many study Bibles. This is *your* exploration, so get your own outline.

Title the various divisions in your outline and write a title for the book.

ROMANS—OUTLINE

A Christian Catechism

I. Doctrine, 1:1–5:21
   - A. Introduction, 1:1-17
   - B. Man's Problem, 1:18–3:20
   - C. God's Solution, 3:21–5:21

II. Implication, 6:1–11:36
   - A. Believers, 6:1–8:39, . . .
      1. and sin, 6:1-23
      2. and the law, 7:1-25
      3. delivered, 8:1-39
   - B. Jews, 9:1–11:36
      1. A sovereign choice, 9:1-33
      2. A universal message, 10:1-21
      3. A future for Israel, 11:1-36

III. Application, 12:1–16:27
   - A. The Believer and the Church, 12:1-21
   - B. The Believer and the World, 13:1-14
   - C. The Believer and Christian Liberty, 14:1–15:7
   - D. Future Plans and Closing Remarks, 15:8–16:27

(O) *Step Five*—Summarize the historical background on the book. You can derive much of this information from the book itself; for some of it you will have to consult Bible study aids, such as, *Zondervan's Pictorial Dictionary of the Bible* (5 volumes), *Eerdmans Bible Handbook,* and *Halley's Bible Handbook.*

Try to determine the following:
1. Who wrote the book? How is the writer presented in the book? What does he reveal about himself?
2. To whom was the book written? Where did they live? What was the geography like and what kind of people were they?
3. When and where was it written? What circumstances and environment surrounded the writer as he wrote?
4. Why was the book written? What was on the writer's mind when he sat down to write? Were there any special problems that occasioned the writing? Is the book designed to communicate a particular thing?

ROMANS—BACKGROUND

1. The letter begins by claiming to be written by Paul (1:1). When the writer describes his ministry later on (Chapter 15), it sounds like Paul. The ideas, style of the letter, and vocabulary all support the claim that Paul wrote it.

   The church fathers and others through the centuries all refer to Paul as the writer.

   Having never visited Rome on his missionary journeys, Paul communicates a warmth and acceptance of the Romans (1:4-12); he states that his contact with them will be *mutually* edifying.

2. Many theories exist as to how the Church at Rome got started (such as, the Apostle Peter founded it), but the best is that it was started by Jews from Rome converted on the day of Pentecost (see Acts 2). Many Jews lived in Rome, having been taken there when Palestine was conquered by Rome in 63 B.C.

3. Paul says he has finished the first phase of his ministry and is ready to move on into Spain (see 15:22). He wants to visit Rome on his way, traveling first to Jerusalem.

   Phoebe is mentioned in this letter (16:1), and she was from Corinth. This, along with other evidence, indicates that Corinth was the city from which Paul wrote Romans. It was written during his third journey, about A.D. 57-58.

4. Since Paul had never ministered in Rome, there were no special problems that confronted him. He wanted to introduce himself to the church and gain their support for his further missionary activity in Spain.

   Some say he wanted to reconcile differences that existed between the Jews and Gentiles, but more probably he simply wanted to set forth a compendium of his thoughts on the theology of the gospel.

(A) *Step Six*—Choose from the possible applications listed in your *Observations* the one on which God would have you work. Suggestions on how to do this are found on pages 215-220.

Do not go to the Advanced section until you have mastered these six basic steps.

Advanced Synthetic Study

If, after doing these steps for a period of time you want to add to your study, you can go two routes. One is to read Chapters 13–16 and implement those parts that apply to these steps. The other is to add further steps of your own. Be bold and imaginative. Try new things. Method is designed to help you, not enslave you. Put aside what doesn't work for you and add what does. The objective of Bible study is to determine the meaning of the writer at the time he wrote it, and apply this truth to your life. Everything else is methodology to help you in this quest. Three more steps are suggested here.

(I) *Step Seven*—Study the format of the book to determine the style the writer uses. The following are examples of what to look for in the book you are studying.

1. Topical—Here the writer deals with certain topics. The Gospel of Matthew is an example. Matthew sets forth the life of Christ in topical fasion.

2. Chronological—Here the writer relates a sequence of events and a story unfolds. An example of this style are in the books of 1 and 2 Kings, which originally were one book.

3. Apologetic—Here in polemic form the writer argues his point. Galatians is a beautiful example of this. Paul dispenses with the usual niceties in his introduction and gets right down to business.

4. Interrogative—Here the writer, in making his point, jabs with probing questions. This is the style used by Malachi.

5. Logical—Here the writer systematically moves in such a way so as to lead us to his conclusion. This is Paul's style in the Book of Romans. He begins with the universal fact of sin, systematically destroying any argument for self-recovery in the process, and leads us to the foot of the cross. His method is that of using questions and answers, much like the techniques used in catechism instruction.

(C) *Step Eight*—Chart the book. This will prove to be a helpful step in viewing the book as a unit and comparing the parts with one another. For assistance in how to do this, turn to Chapter 15, pages 189-214. Study the example in Figure 8.

(I) *Step Nine*—Determine the place of the book in the Bible as a whole. Each book has its own unique contribution to the whole of the Bible. What would be missing if this book were omitted?

ROMANS – A CHRISTIAN CATECHISM

	Doctrine									Implication			Application			
Reference	1:1-17	1:18-2:16	2:17-3:20	3:21-31	4:1-25	5:1-21	6:1-23	7:1-25	8:1-39	9:1-33	10:1-21	11:1-36	12:1-21	13:1-14	14:1-15:7	15:8-16:27
Section	Introduction	The Unbeliever and Sin	The Unbeliever and the Law	The Unbeliever Delivered	Deliverance in the OT III. — Abraham	The Doctrine of Imputation Elaborated	The Believer and Sin	The Believer and the Law	The Believer Delivered	A Sovereign Choice	A Universal Message	A Future for Israel	The Believer and the Church	The Believer and the World	The Believer and Christian Liberty	Future Plans and Closing Remarks
Theme	SIN			SALVATION			SANCTIFICATION			SELECTION			SERVICE			
	MAN Unbeliever in Sin			GOD (God the Son)			MAN-GOD (HS) Believer in Sin			GOD (God the Father)			MAN			
				LIFE BY FAITH									SERVICE BY FAITH			
	Slave to Sin						Slave to God						Slave Serving God			
	HIS Righteousness IN LAW			HIS Righteousness IMPUTED			HIS Righteousness OBEYED			HIS Righteousness IN ELECTION			HIS Righteousness DISPLAYED			
	The Need of Salvation			The Way of Salvation			The Life of Salvation			The Scope of Salvation			The Service of Salvation			

Figure 8

ROMANS—ITS CONTRIBUTION

Many believe Romans to be the greatest of the New Testament books. It certainly is the most thorough presentation of the "whole counsel of God." It forms the basis of the great theological works written through the ages and it was the major book of the Protestant Reformation.

In contrast to the other religions of the world, which are religions of achievement, Christianity is a religion of rescue. Romans is the clearest presentation of this fact of all the New Testament documents.

Conclusion

Ideally the synthetic method should be used in conjunction with the analytic method. View the book as a whole, then look at its parts, and finally reexamine the whole. Diagramed, it would look like this:

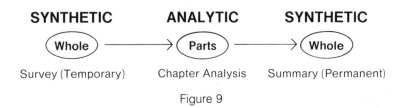

Figure 9

Applying this method means you do a synthetic study first, as described in this chapter. Then do a chapter by chapter analysis of the book described in the preceding chapter. Finally, repeat the synthetic study of the book. This final study will either confirm or invalidate the first synthetic study.

If you elect to do this, be careful to approach your second synthetic study with an open, fresh mind. Put your first study aside and don't refer to it till you are all done. Then bring it out for purposes of comparison.

This is a step that should only be taken by a seasoned Bible student. Do not tackle more than you can handle, as it leads to frustration, discouragement, and ultimately quitting. If, as you implement these steps, you find you are doing too much, back away from the new material. You are not in competition with anyone. Later, if you feel up to it, give it another try. If you decide never to try, fine!

10 The Topical Method of Bible Study

<table>
<tr><td>

TOPICAL STUDY

The tracing of a selected topic through the Bible or a portion of it.

</td></tr>
</table>

In Paul's Epistle to the Romans he introduces a number of different topics and weaves them together into the message he is communicating. Examples of these topics are faith, grace, justification, Holy Spirit, and sin. His treatment of each of these topics is not complete, but it does give you some insights into how God feels about them.

This is true for all the writers of the Bible. Each touches on a host of topics in making his point.

In the topical method of Bible study you "chase" a selected topic through the Bible. How far you chase it will depend on the time you have and your overall objective. For the average student, the larger the topic the more narrow the study will have to be.

For example, the study of *sin* in the Bible would promise to be a gargantuan task. Even a study of *Jesus' teaching on sin* would be huge. Either you will have to avoid subjects of this size, or narrow them down still further, like, *John's teaching of sin in his first letter*.

A smaller topic can be treated much more broadly. If, for example, you decide to study the word *victory* in the Bible, you can search all 66 books, and find that in the whole Bible it only appears 11 times.

Sometimes the topic being studied has synonyms: law, statutes, commands, ordinances, precepts, testimonies are all used interchangeably in the Psalms. For this reason, a topical or cyclopedic index can often prove more useful than a concordance. The *Thompson Chain Reference Bible* is excellent for this, as is Thomas Nelson's *The Open Bible* Edition. *Strong's* and *Young's* concordances are two exhaustive ones from which to choose. *Nave's Topical Bible* is still another.

As in the Verse Analysis method, to draw attention to the four basic parts of Bible study, a letter indicating the part you are doing is noted next to each of the steps.

    (O) OBSERVATION
    (I) INTERPRETATION
    (C) CORRELATION
    (A) APPLICATION

Basic Topical Study

For purposes of illustration, we will use the word *hospitality* as our topic for study.

(C) *Step One*—Choose the word to be studied and the boundaries of the study, such as a book, section of Bible, or the whole Bible. Write out the purpose or objective of the study. Using a Bible study aid such as those listed above, locate the references to be included in your study. On a sheet of paper list these references vertically using the left hand side of the sheet.

HOSPITALITY—TOPIC, PURPOSE, AND REFERENCES

Topic to Be Studied: HOSPITALITY

Purpose of the Study: To learn the biblical concept of hospitality, so that we might use our home as the Bible teaches.

References:

>   Matthew 25:35
>   Luke 7:44-46
>   Luke 11:5-8
>   Romans 12:13
>   1 Timothy 3:2
>   Titus 1:8
>   Hebrews 13:2
>   1 Peter 4:9

(O) *Step Two*—Take a sheet of paper and mark *Observations* on the top. This will be used throughout the study. Include on this sheet:

1. Observations—Note any and every detail you notice. Bombard the references with questions such as: who? what? where? when? why? and how? Note the nouns, verbs, and other key words.

2. Problems—Write out what you don't understand about the references and topic. Don't say, "I don't understand Ephesians 4:8." Rather, elaborate on what it is you don't understand. Some of your questions will resolve themselves as you continue your study. Others will be resolved only by referring to outside sources such as your pastor or a commentary. Some of your questions may never be answered.

3. Possible application—you will observe several of these in the course of your study. Note them on this sheet with an **(A)** in the margin. At the conclusion of your study you will return to these possible applications and select the one on which the Holy Spirit will have you focus.

HOSPITALITY—OBSERVATIONS

(O) • *Definitions:* Hospitality is "the reception and entertainment of strangers" *(The Open Bible).*

Hospitable as entered in the dictionary listing is between *Hospice,* a place for a stranger to rest and lodge, and *Hospital,* a place to care for the sick. It means: "Given to generous and cordial reception of guests" *(Webster's New Collegiate Dictionary).*

Hospitality is "hospitable treatment, reception, or disposition" *(Webster's New Collegiate Dictionary).*

(O) • Matthew 25:35—Jesus' judgment on the nations for their acceptance or rejection of Him and His brethren in the context of provision.

—The bare essentials are listed: food, drink, shelter, clothing, and fellowship.

—Why is the emphasis placed on strangers? The church was dispersed and the traveling believer could find acceptance and provision in the context of the local body of believers; therefore, the saints were to expect strangers. Also they never knew when they might be entertaining angels (Hebrews 13:2).

(A) —My tendency is to entertain those I *know,* rather than provide for the stranger.

(O) • Luke 7:44-46—Jesus contrasts the entertaining host and the hospitable stranger. The host did not provide any courtesies to his guest, while the stranger provided water, greeting, and anointing.

—Jesus reveals that a person's motives are reflected in whether hospitality is given out of love or obligation.

—What are the courtesies of hospitality in my culture today? A welcome greeting, something to drink, communicating an interest in the guest, food, and other amenities.

—Contrast Simon to Martha and Mary, who eagerly received Jesus into their home (Luke 10:38; John 12:2).

(O) • Luke 11:5-8—There is a cost in meeting the needs of others: inconvenience (the hour was late and the family settled for the night), time, and provision.

—Because of a friendship (relationship), the person felt free to go to him for help in a time of need.

—Hospitality is meeting the needs of others, not merely entertaining guests as our culture portrays. Cultural entertaining to show off our skills as cooks, tidy homekeepers, or the array of such things as china, silver, and art objects, is opposite of the biblical teaching on hospitality.

(O) • Romans 12:13—The providing of needs and the commitment to hospitality are listed together.

—The believers are singled out as the recipients.

—Synonyms: given, committed, addicted (1 Corinthians 16:15 KJV).

—Hospitality isn't a decision making procedure but the reflection of a life style. The home isn't regarded as an ivory tower of retreat for themselves but a hospice for service to others.

(O) • 1 Timothy 3:2—What does it mean to be given to hospitality? The word *given* connotes more than something you take or leave, but a way of life, a life style.

—In Genesis 18, Sarah and Abraham were not expecting guests, yet as the strangers approached, Abraham *ran* to meet them, greeted them by *bowing* to them, gave them *water* to wash their feet, and then had Sarah prepare a full meal. They went out of their way to make the strangers welcome. The cost to them was time, effort, and provisions. Yet there was no hesitation on their part, but an eager giving of themselves (see 2 Corinthians 8:5).

(O) • Titus 1:8—Church leaders must love hospitality.

—Hospitality cannot be separated from people and a concern and interest in them. It means giving myself to others because I am concerned for them.

(O) —In John 4, we see Jesus as a tired, hungry traveler. Yet He gave Himself to the Samaritan woman by talking with her, answering her questions, and offering her living water that would satisfy the deepest needs of her life. What a contrast to the response of the disciples, who were shocked that he would even speak to her!

(O) —2 Kings 4:8-10—A Shunammite couple with financial means prepared a room with a table, stool, lamp, and bed for the traveling prophet Elisha, so he might have a place to stay.

(A) • Hebrews 13:2—It is easy to become so involved in my own activities and friends that I neglect the stranger, such as visitors who attend church without my greeting them. If I did my part along with the rest of the congregation, "official greeters" wouldn't be necessary.

    —Do angels still visit today?

    —What are the Bible's accounts of people entertaining angels and not realizing who they were?

        • Genesis 18:2-15—Abraham
        • Genesis 19:1-22—Lot
        • Judges 6:11-24—Gideon
        • Judges 13:1-21—Samson's mother and father

    —The angelic visitations were to convey a message, yet in each account they were entertained not because they were angels but because the people opened their homes and lives to strangers.

(O)(C) • 1 Peter 4:9—Because hospitality involves giving, the admonition of 2 Corinthians 9:7 applies: "Each person should give what he has decided in his heart to give, not reluctantly or under compulsion, for God loves a cheerful giver."

    —Hospitality should reflect a heart attitude of eagerness, not the fulfillment of a duty. If I grasp the privilege of ministering to others by being hospitable, it removes the obligation and allows the Spirit of God to minister to others through me, which then becomes the reflection of a life style.

(I) *Step Three*—On the sheet used in *Step One* write out the *key thought* for each reference listed. The key thought is the distilled essence or main idea of the verse stated in your own words.

While doing *Step Three,* you should list many of your *observations* suggested in *Step Two*.

HOSPITALITY—KEY THOUGHTS

Topic to Be Studied: HOSPITALITY
Purpose of the Study: To learn the biblical concept of hospitality, so that we might use our home as the Bible teaches.
References:

Matthew 25:35—acceptance and provision for the stranger
Luke 7:44-46—to provide the courtesies of hospitality
Luke 11:5-8—cost involved in meeting others' needs
Romans 12:13—providing needs; committed to hospitality
1 Timothy 3:2—church leaders must be committed to hospitality
Titus 1:8—a lover of hospitality
Hebrews 13:2—entertain strangers; some have hosted angels
1 Peter 4:9—be hospitable without grudging

(C) *Step Four*—Arrange the verses into categories. The *key thoughts* listed in *Step Three* will help you select your categories. Ask yourself questions like, *What are the main categories suggested by these verses? How would I outline this subject to another person?* Some verses will fit under more than one category.

HOSPITALITY—CATEGORIES

Attitudes of hospitality
    1 Peter 4:9; Titus 1:8; 1 Timothy 3:2; Romans 12:13
Definition of hospitality
    Matthew 25:35; Luke 7:44-46; Romans 12:13
Costs and rewards of hospitality
    Luke 11:5-8; Hebrews 13:2

(C) *Step Five*—Outline the categories created in *Step Four*, listing the major divisions and important subdivisions. Place the key verses next to each division and subpoint.

Work for logical order and simplicity of structure. Don't make it complicated. Generally speaking, the simpler you make it the more you understand it. Constantly keep in mind the purpose of the study.

HOSPITALITY—OUTLINE

  I. Hospitality defined (Romans 12:13; Matthew 25:35-40)
 II. Hospitality demonstrated (Luke 7:44-46)
      A. Attitudes toward hospitality (Titus 1:8, 1 Peter 4:9; 1 Timothy 3:2)
      B. Costs and benefits of hospitality (Luke 11:5-8; Hebrews 13:2)

(I) *Step Six*—Write out the *key thought* for each major division, remembering that the key thought is your stating the main idea in one sentence. Then write a key thought for the whole study. This becomes the "big idea" or theme of the study. In the process, you narrow down the material (as in a funnel) from the key thought of each verse to the key thought of the whole.

HOSPITALITY—KEY THOUGHTS OF THE WHOLE STUDY

  I. Hospitality defined:
     Being sensitive to the needs of people around me, including the stranger, and providing the necessary aid to meet those needs.
 II. Hospitality demonstrated:
     By fulfilling the common courtesies in my culture so the guest knows he is welcome.
      A. An attitude of commitment and love for hospitality is essential.
      B. Time, effort, and provisions are part of the cost, but the benefits can be an unexpected heavenly guest.

Key Thought for the Whole Study: Hospitality is committing myself to others, including the stranger, and communicating a genuine interest in them by extending cultural courtesies and providing for their needs.

(A) *Step Seven*—Choose from the possible applications listed in your *Observations* the one on which God would have you work.

HOSPITALITY—APPLICATION

I attend a large church where it is easy to become lost among the people. I don't go out of my way to greet people I don't recognize. I merely go on my own way.

This is contrary to the Bible's teaching of having a life style of being hospitable.

I will try to greet those around me following the worship service, introduce myself, and inquire if they're visitors. I'll welcome them and ask if I can be of any service to them (such as, finding a Sunday School class).

Advanced Topical Study

The following additional steps are optional and should only be tried after you have gained proficiency in the first part of the study. This cannot be overemphasized: don't try to tackle too much at once. Add to your methodology slowly. You are seeking to develop life-long habits of Bible study.

(I) *Step Eight*—Take the key thought of your study and write several paragraphs elaborating on the central truth. View this key thought as the pivotal point of your elaboration. Never stray far from it. The purpose here is to nail down the basic truths or principles found in the study.

Hospitality—Elaborating on the Key Thought

Hospitality is committing myself to others, including the stranger, and communicating a genuine interest in them by extending cultural courtesies and providing for their needs.

Hospitality is a commitment in that it is not merely entertaining but a way of life—a lifestyle. Entertaining is something you choose to do or don't do depending on your will, but hospitality is an openness of life and home. It is giving of yourself to others in an attitude of commitment, not obligation.

Hospitality is communicating to your guest an interest in him by extending common courtesies in keeping with our culture. This might include a warm handshake, the offering of a beverage, time to converse (without mentally being preoccupied as you listen), and the invitation to a meal or lodging if it is appropriate to the time of day and circumstances.

The guest may have needs other than physical (such as, food and drink). These may include acceptance or a problem which needs to be discussed. Hospitality includes fellowship with genuine interest in seeking to minister to the needs of the other person.

Because hospitality involves giving, there is a cost involved. It could be in time, effort, or material things, yet the cost is only one aspect of hospitality. The other is the reward of hospitality. This may or may not be evident immediately. God is a giving God and when His children participate in His nature, He rewards them, sometimes with a "heavenly" guest.

Therefore, by committing myself to others, including the stranger, and communicating a genuine interest in them by extending cultural courtesies and providing for their needs, I am obeying the biblical admonition of being hospitable.

(C) *Step Nine*—Referring to the material found in Chapter 15, pages 189-214, make a chart on your topical study. This will be a helpful step in viewing the study as a whole and seeing how the parts relate to one another. The type of topical study you have done will influence the kind of chart you select.

HOSPITALITY — CHART

BIBLICAL HOSPITALITY	CULTURAL ENTERTAINING
Reflection of a lifestyle	Fulfilling an obligation
Sharing what you have	Showing off what you have
Stranger is welcome	The well-known person is welcome
Home as a hospice	Home as an ivory tower

Figure 10

(I) *Step Ten*—Refer to outside material on the topic you studied and add or alter any part of your study. This last step is a helpful "check" on your conclusions, especially if you plan on any public presentation of your study.

The Biographical Method of Bible Study

This is a "fun" kind of Bible study, for you have an opportunity to explore the characters of people the Holy Spirit has placed in the Bible and learn from their lives. Paul, writing to the Corinthians, said, "These things happened to them as examples and were written down as warnings for us, on whom the fulfillment of the ages has come" (1 Corinthians 10:11).

A great deal of material has been written on some of the people in the Bible. When you study people like Jesus, Abraham, and

Moses, you may want to narrow down your study to areas such as, "The life of Jesus as revealed in John's Gospel," "Moses during the Exodus," or "What the New Testament says about Abraham." Constantly work at keeping your Bible studies to manageable size.

The same reference materials suggested in Chapter 10 (page 138) are useful here.

As in the Verse Analysis method, a letter indicating the part you are doing has been noted next to each of the steps to draw attention to the four basic parts of Bible study.

(O) OBSERVATION
(I) INTERPRETATION
(C) CORRELATION
(A) APPLICATION

Basic Biographical Study

For the purpose of illustration, we will use Rahab in this study.

(C) *Step One*—Choose the person you want to study and set the boundaries of the study (for example, "The life of David before he became king"). Using a concordance or cyclopedic index, locate the references that have to do with the person you are studying. Read these several times, and write a summary for each.

RAHAB—REFERENCES

Joshua   2:1—a harlot living in Jericho

2:3—the king of Jericho asks about the spies from her

2:4—she hid the spies and lied to the king

2:5—she purposely distracted the men of the city

2:6—she hid the spies under flax

2:8-9—she acknowledged that the Lord had conquered Jericho

> 2:10—the rumor of the Exodus and victory over the Amorites
>
> 2:11—the fear of her people and the fact that the Lord was God of all
>
> 2:12-13—she asked for safety for herself and her family
>
> 2:14—the spies make her a promise
>
> 2:15—she provided their escape route
>
> 2:16—she gave them a plan for safety
>
> 2:17-20—the spies plan for her safety
>
> 2:21—the sign of her commitment
>
> 6:22-23—Rahab's rescue along with her family

Matthew   1:5—Rahab's place in the genealogy of Jesus Christ

Hebrews   11:31—by faith she didn't die because she received the spies

James   2:25—she was justified by her action of sending the spies away

(O) *Step Two*—Take a sheet of paper and mark *OBSERVATIONS* on the top. Use this sheet throughout the study. Include on this page:

1. Observations—Note any and every detail you notice about this person. Who was he? What did he do? Where did he live? When did he live? Why did he do what he did? How did he accomplish it? Note details about him and his character.

2. Problems—Write out what you don't understand about this person and events in his life.

3. Possible application—Mark several of these during the course of your study, and write an (A) in the margin. At the conclusion of your study, you will return to these possible applications and select the one on which the Holy Spirit will have you focus.

(No illustration is included here, for the process is the same as *Step Two* under the *Topical Method of Bible Study*, pages 139-143.)

(O) *Step Three*—In paragraph form, write a brief sketch of the person's life. Include the important events and characteristics stating the facts without interpretation. Keep the material as chronological as possible.

RAHAB—A SKETCH OF HER LIFE

Rahab was a harlot in the town of Jericho, which was situated across the Jordan River in the land of Canaan. She, along with other members of her community, had heard how God had allowed the Israelites to cross the Red Sea on dry land and how they had also defeated the two kings of the Amorites.

When the spies came to her door she received them in peace and hid them from the king of Jericho, who was seeking their lives. She lied to the king that they were not there and sent the men of the city on a false chase after them.

She requested of the spies safety for herself and her family testifying to them that she believed the Israelite God to be the God of heaven and earth based on what she had heard of His acts.

The spies promised her safety if she wouldn't reveal their whereabouts and have all her family in her house when they conquered Jericho. Proof of their mutual commitment was a scarlet cord hanging from her window.

Her life was spared at the fall of Jericho and later she is found as the great great grandmother of King David and thus in the lineage of Jesus Christ.

The New Testament also records her faith and justification by her act of receiving the spies.

(I) *Step Four*—List the strengths and weaknesses of the person. Why did God consider him/her great? When did he or she fall short?

RAHAB—STRENGTHS AND WEAKNESSES

Strengths: Based on very little knowledge (a rumor), Rahab staked her whole life and the lives of her family on what she heard. She *applied* what she knew. God considers this greatness—to believe Him and act on what you have. Her people had the same information, yet they didn't believe.
Weaknesses: She was a liar and a traitor to her country.

(I) *Step Five*—Choose the key verse for his/her life. This is the verse or passage that more than any other sums up the direction of that person's life. State the crowning achievement or contribution of that life.

RAHAB—KEY VERSE

"By faith the prostitute Rahab because she welcomed the spies, was not killed with those who were disobedient" (Hebrews 11:31).

Her faith was exercised while she was a prostitute and God counts her great at that stage of her life, not following her acceptance into the Jewish community. She acted on the little knowledge she had by hiding the spies and believed that Jehovah was the true God of heaven and earth.

(I) *Step Six*—In one sentence, state the key thought regarding the person's life. This may be positive or negative. Here you are trying to sum up the person's life in one sentence. There should be a correlation between this key thought and the key verse in *Step Five*.

RAHAB—KEY THOUGHT

Rahab was willing to take great risks with God on the basis of little information, and God considered this true greatness.

(A) *Step Seven*—Choose from the possible applications listed in your *Observations* the one on which God would have you work.

RAHAB—APPLICATION

It is easy to fall into the habit of reading the Bible to gain new insights and miss the life-changing aspects of application. I am guilty of this.

Since the key to a changed life is applying the Word of God to my life, not increasing my knowledge, I will pray and commit myself to apply a truth of Scripture each time I read the Bible.

Advanced Biographical Study

The following steps may be added if and when you feel they will help in your biographical studies. They are optional and should only be included progressively as you gain confidence and proficiency.

(O) *Step Eight*—Trace the historical background of the person. Use a Bible dictionary to augment this step only when necessary. The following questions should stimulate your thinking.

1. When did the person live? What were the political, social, religious, and economic conditions of his time?
2. Where was the person born? Who were his parents? Was there anything unusual surrounding his birth and childhood?
3. What was his vocation? Was he a teacher, farmer, or in some other occupation? Did this influence his later ministry? How?
4. Who was his spouse? Did they have any children? What were they like? Did they help or hinder his life and ministry?
5. Chart the person's travels. Where did he/she go? Why? What was accomplished?
6. How did the person die? Was there anything extraordinary in his life?

RAHAB—HISTORICAL BACKGROUND

Jericho, the City of Palms, was in the land of Canaan. It was on a caravan route between Egypt to the south and Babylon to the north. Canaan consisted of small kingdoms, each with fortified cities and a king (see Joshua 9:1-2). Jericho was fortified with a double wall, and Rahab's house was on that wall.

The Canaanites were the descendants of Ham (see Genesis 19:18-25), and their worship consisted of idolatry, fertility rites, and human sacrifices to Baal.

From the time the residents of Jericho heard of the Exodus, they lived in fear. The men of the city had hearts that "melted" within them.

According to the Bible account, the flax had been harvested since it was on the roof to dry, thereby setting the story in the end of March or first of April.

Later Rahab married Salmon and had a son, Boaz. Boaz married the Gentile Ruth, after whom the Old Testament book is named. Their son Obed bore Jesse, who was the father of Israel's greatest king, David.

(I) *Step Nine*—Write a couple of paragraphs on the person's philosophy of life. What motivated him or her? What were his or her attitudes? What were his or her life objectives? What did the person want out of life and did he or she get it?

RAHAB—PHILOSOPHY OF LIFE

Rahab's philosophy of life was to believe that the God of the Israelites must be the true and living God. She had heard of the miracles He had performed for His people. While her countrymen lived in fear, she lived in faith, believing that God had already conquered Jericho. Her faith motivated her to receive the spies, hide them, and help them escape. She also wanted safety for herself and her family, which she received. She acquired a permanent place in the history of Israel and in the lineage of Jesus Christ.

(C) *Step Ten*—Referring to the material in Chapter 15, pages 189-214, make a chart on this person. Make it chronological, marking the various phases of his or her life. If you desire, make another chart showing his or her relationship to others who entered his or her life. Figure 10 is an illustration of the life of Rahab in chart form.

RAHAB - CHART

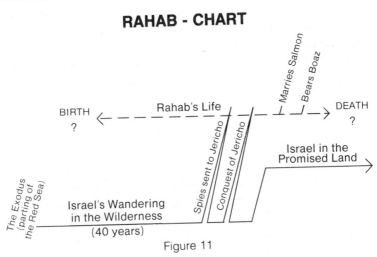

Figure 11

(C) *Step Eleven*—Compare and/or contrast the person with others in the Bible. The person compared may be a contemporary, or if it is someone like Moses or Abraham, the comparison may be made with Christ.

RAHAB—COMPARISON

An interesting comparison to Rahab is Lot's wife. She had a family relationship with Abraham and was aware of God's promises to him. Yet when the angels came to deliver her from the destruction of Sodom and gave specific commands not to look back, she didn't believe. This unbelief resulted in her judgment as she turned into a pillar of salt.

Chapter 13–16 have been added to further stimulate your mind in expanding your biographical study and making it an even greater challenge to you. Just as it isn't necessary to include all of the above eleven steps in your study, so also don't feel that you need to incorporate all the suggestions in Chapters 13–16. They simply give you an opportunity to create your own personal study from a variety of ideas. Experiment till the method maximizes your ability to glean from your Bible study what you want.

III Improving Your Bible Study Skills

12 Improvement Is for Everyone

Section III will help you improve the skills that you have already learned and launch you into developing your own methods of doing Bible study. Before you use the methods suggested here, however, make sure you are familiar with the methods described in Section II of this book. After you have done the Bible studies described there for some time, using those methods, refer to this part.

The contents of this section will help you go into greater depth into the four major essentials or parts of Bible study—observation, interpretation, correlation, and application. As you begin to sense the need for some additional help in a particular part of your Bible study, or want some new ideas, refer to the appropriate part.

This section will teach you new concepts of Bible study as well as new methods. Take sufficient time to understand any new concepts thoroughly. You will want to employ these in any of the methods you use, i.e., analytical, synthetic, topical, etc.

The suggestions in this section are only a sampling of the hundreds that are available. Use your own creativity to develop new methods, but before you do, take time to learn the methods presented. True creativity follows structure.

13 Observation: The Role of a Detective

OBSERVATION
The recording of what may be seen in a selected method of Bible study.

Webster's New Collegiate Dictionary defines observation as the "act of recognizing and noting a fact or occurrence"; it means to be mentally aware of what one sees. The purpose of observation in Bible study is to saturate yourself with the content of the passage of Scripture, to become as familiar as possible with all that the biblical writer is saying and implying.

Accuracy is important in observation. Not everything you read will be of equal value in ascertaining the meaning of the passage. So you will have to learn to discern what is important and what is not. Practice and concentration are the two ingredients that will sharpen your expertise.

Jesus' last words of instruction to His disciples were to prepare them for the time when He would no longer be physically with them. He assured them that "the Counselor, the Holy Spirit, whom the Father will send in my name, will *teach* you all things and will remind you of everything I have said to you" (John 14:26). A little later on in the same conversation He said, "But when He, the Spirit of truth, comes, He will *guide* you into all truth" (John 16:13).

A prayerful dependence on the Holy Spirit is key to all aspects of Bible study, and especially to observation. Diligence, openness, dependence, an eagerness to learn—all these must characterize the student as he begins digging in the Word.

How do you begin observing? Where do you start? Take a piece of paper (8½" x 11" will do fine) and begin to record all you see. No item or idea is insignificant. Write it down so your mind can free itself to look for new things. The following list is not necessarily given in the order of their importance. You will want to pick and choose from them depending on your level of proficiency and the type of material you are studying. Some suggestions will be more applicable to a character study, for example, than to an analytic study.

Have the Right Mental Attitude

You have already learned that a basic requirement for making good observations is a prayerful dependence on the Holy Spirit. As you have worked on making good observations, you have probably become aware that more is required than just that attitude. Five more requirements are necessary as well.

1. *Observation requires an act of the will.* You must have the will and the desire to be aware of what is in the biblical text, then to perceive and recognize what is there. You must have the determination to know and to learn. For example, when you meet people for the first time, do you remember their names? If not, it is likely that you have not purposed in your mind that you are going to learn their names. Learning begins with an act of the will—you must want to learn.

2. *Observation requires a persistence to know.* Learning is never easy. It requires diligence and discipline. You cannot have an effective disciple without him or her being a disciplined person. One of the keys in persisting in your personal Bible study is to see that the results are really worth the effort and the work that you have put into it. Take time to reflect on the results that have taken place in your life over the past six months because you have been doing Bible study faithfully.

3. *Observation requires patience.* In a day when you have instant communication, instant everything, there is a tendency to want an instant education. True learning, however, takes a great deal of time. You cannot take shortcuts in the learning process. The so-called short cuts are in fact only short circuits; they lead to ineffective results. In personal Bible study as well as in everything else in the Christian life, the process is as important as the product.

4. *Observation requires diligent recording.* As you look over the observations you recorded in some of your previous Bible studies, you will probably notice that there are some that you have completely forgotten. You will remember only a small portion of the observations you had made. So it is best for you to record all the observations you make in your personal Bible study diligently. In doing so, you will again see the importance and value of having a study Bible where you can keep a record of your good observations for the next time you study that portion of Scripture.

5. *Observation requires caution.* Observation is only the first step in studying the Bible—interpretation, correlation, and application must follow. Three warnings must be heeded.

    a. Don't lose yourself in the details; divide your time proportionately for all parts of the passage under study.

    b. Don't stop with observations, but go on to ask questions and seek meaningful answers.

    c. Don't give equal weight to everything; carefully discern what is more important.

Use the Six Basic Questions

1. *WHO?* List all the people involved. In 1 Thessalonians 1 you will note that Paul talks about *we, you,* and *they.* In verse 1 the *we* included Paul, Silas, and Timothy. The same verse also suggests that *you* refers to the believers in the city of Thessalonica. Verse 7 reveals who is included in the *they*—those in the provinces of Macedonia and Achaia.

2. *WHAT?* What happened? What ideas are expressed? What are the results? In 1 Thessalonians 1 Paul is discussing the effects of the gospel. The Thessalonians' labor was not in vain: lives were changed (verse 5). The Thessalonian believers assumed responsibility for sharing the Good News with others (verse 8). Paul could see from his "spiritual grandchildren" the results of his ministry to the Thessalonians (verses 9-10).

3. *WHERE?* Where does this take place? What is the geographical setting? Here a good Bible dictionary will prove helpful: Zondervan's *Pictorial Dictionary of the Bible* is a good investment if you don't already own a similar volume. As you investigate the background of this city, you discover that it was rebuilt and given its name in 315 B.C. at the time of Alexander the Great. It was named after Alexander's step-sister. Located in the northeastern corner of the Thermaic Gulf (here you will want to consult your maps), it straddled the Egnation Way, a famous road in Macedonia used by the Romans. The city had the best natural harbor in Macedonia. During Paul's time it was the capital of that province. Many additional similar observations could be made.

4. *WHEN?* When did this take place? What was the historical background? Consulting your Bible dictionary once again, you discover that Paul founded the church in Thessalonica on his second missionary journey (see Acts 17:1-9). After ministering in this city, Paul and his team worked their way south through the Greek provinces of Macedonia and Achaia ending up in Corinth. It was from that city that Paul wrote 1 Thessalonians in about A.D. 54.

5. *WHY?* Why did this happen? What is the purpose or stated reason? Continuing to use 1 Thessalonians as our example, we find by reading the historical account of Paul's second journey (Acts 17–18) that he was plagued by a group of unbelieving Jews. These men followed Paul from city to city causing trouble. Persecutions of the new Christians inevitably followed. Timothy was sent back to Thessalonica to see how the believers fared and to encourage them in their Christian lives. Timothy returned with a positive report and Paul followed up with this letter. His purpose in writing was to communicate his confidence in them, assure them of the hope of the resurrection (a particularly precious doctrine during times of persecution), and exhort them to holy living.

6. *HOW?* How are things accomplished? How well? How quickly? By what method? Paul followed up his ministry to the Thessalonians by sending Timothy back to see them and then writing this letter. Though Paul had ministered there but a short time, the Thessalonian believers had become committed disciples of Christ.

Discover the Form or Structure of the Passage Under Study

As you observe the contents of a passage you are studying, you will also want to become aware of the form it takes. How God says something is as important as what He says. You should ask yourself questions like, *How does the writer deal with the content? What form or structure does he use?* Some examples you may notice are:

- The writer asks four questions and answers them.
- The writer lists seventeen things we are to avoid.
- The writer gives us five commands we are to obey.
- The writer makes three declarative statements and then supports them.

The writer of a section of Scripture may place his content in the form of poetry, narrative, parable, logical argument, discourse, practical advice, history, drama, or some other forms. The way that the content of God's Word unfolds reveals the mind and method of the writer in communicating God's truth, and gives you further insight and feeling into the meaning of the passage under study. Some other things to look for as you examine structure are:

- Use of cause and effect (as in 1 Thessalonians 1)
- The movement from particulars to generalities (as in 1 Thessalonians 2), or from generalities to particulars (as in 1 Thessalonians 5)
- Use of Old Testament references in the New Testament (as in Romans 10)
- Use of illustrations in the text of the main argument or narrative (as in Galatians 4)
- Use of the current events of the times (as in Luke 13:1-5)

Some of the methods writers employ to relate their messages are:

1. *Relating the way things are*—1 Thessalonians 1 is a good example of this. Paul is communicating certain truths in this passage, but he does that by reviewing a sequence of events they all had in common. We might paraphrase this chapter as follows: "I came to you, preached the gospel, and you responded. This response manifested itself in your sharing the gospel with those near you. Their response to the gospel assured me that you were serious in your commitment to Christ."

2. *Admonition or exhortation*—Paul's letter to the Galatians illustrates this. The Galatians had bought the message of the Judaizers. Paul exhorts them to consider the implications of following what he considers grievous error. In Galatians 2:1-14 Paul relates *the way things are* as he does in 1 Thessalonians 1, but this is parenthetical and illustrative of the main argument he is setting forth. Commands to obey and errors to avoid are the kinds of things to look for in this type of passage.

3. *Teaching*—Jesus' dissertation commonly referred to as the Sermon on the Mount (Matthew 5–7), and Paul's Epistle to the Romans are examples of the teaching style of communication. The

message is timeless in that the author is not addressing a current situation as Paul does in his letter to the Galatians. In Romans, Paul uses a common technique of teaching: asking questions and then answering them. For example, he asks the question, "What advantage, then, is there in being a Jew, or what value is there in circumcision?" (Romans 3:1). Then he proceeds to answer his own questions, much like a catechism.

4. *Parables*—These are frequently used by Jesus as a poignant way of driving home spiritual truth. With parables, the student seeks to discover the main point being made and must be careful not to allow his imagination to carry him to conclusions not intended by the story. Particularly with parables, it is possible to observe too much.

5. *Narrative*—Large portions of the Bible take this form of writing. Genesis, Exodus, most of Numbers, Joshua through Esther, most of the Gospels and Acts are all narrative in form.

6. *Other methods*—Practical advice is found in Proverbs and various poetic styles in the Psalms, other poetical books, and many of the prophetical books. As you begin your study, note the form or structure carefully, for it will greatly assist you in identifying the means used by the writer in communicating his message.

Find the Key Words

In some passages that you study, the key word jumps out at you and is readily apparent. *Love* in 1 Corinthians 13 and *faith* in Hebrews 11 are examples of this. Most of the time, however, it requires diligent work to discover the key words in a passage.

While Webster's dictionary is helpful in defining the English words of a Bible passage, it is inadequate in giving the literal meanings of Hebrew or Greek words or phrases. To check the definition of a biblical word, the average person must rely on other resources. Often a Bible dictionary will give a more thorough and comprehensive description of a word or topic.

Other background material which will prove helpful in defining

New Testament words are W. E. Vine's *An Expository Dictionary of New Testament Words* and M. R. Vincent's *Word Studies in the New Testament. Girdlestone's Old Testament Synonyms* is a good reference for Old Testament word studies. Good commentaries, explaining the literal meaning of biblical words and phrases, will also be helpful. Without a command of either the Hebrew or Greek languages, you can profit in your study of the Scriptures from the excellent scholarship and research available in a few well chosen books.

Let us take 1 Peter 1 as our example. In the *King James Version,* Peter says, "that the trial of your faith" (verse 7). As you compare the word *trial* with the *Revised Standard Version,* you note that it is replaced with the word *genuineness.* The *New International Version* uses the phrase *proved genuine.* James Strong's *Exhaustive Concordance of the Bible* will give you the Greek word and the other places in the Bible where that same Greek word is used: Luke 14:19; 1 Corinthians 3:13; 2 Corinthians 8:22; 1 Thessalonians 2:4; and James 1:3, 12. And you find the word is used in a variety of ways.

Tracing the meaning of this Greek word *dokimos,* you find it means, "A test, the means of proof, the result of the contact of faith with trial, and hence the verification of faith" (Vincent's *Word Studies*). This is a key idea, not only in 1 Peter 1, but in the whole of his first epistle. These dispersed Christians were suffering for their faith. The difficulties were not without benefit, however. They revealed that their faith in Christ was genuine. Like gold purified by fire, the suffering Christian is "tested in battle and found to be pure and reliable." *Suffering* is one of the major themes in 1 Peter and *trial* (KJV) is a key word in understanding that suffering.

In Romans 3 words like *propitiation, justified, remission, redemption, righteousness,* and *forbearance* (KJV) are all key in understanding the meaning of this passage.

If you feel that your level of understanding of words such as these is small, and that such study is, at best, difficult, don't feel as though you are alone. These illustrations are meant to be suggestive of how you can go about studying a passage. Use what you feel comfortable with and leave the rest. At a later time when you feel comfortable with the tools you are using in your study, you will be ready to go back and add a few more.

Consider Comparisons and Contrasts

Two kinds of observations to make in your personal Bible study are comparisons and contrasts. Comparisons show how things are alike; contrasts show how things are different. Make a special effort to find contrasts and comparisons in the passage you are studying. If there are none in that passage, try to find other Scriptures which will give you contrasts and comparisons with the section you are studying.

To help you in making observations of comparison and contrast, look for words like "even so," "as . . . so . . .," and "likewise." These are not the *only* words that provide comparisons, but they almost always do so. When you find a comparison, spend sufficient time thinking through on the things being compared. Then record as many ways as possible in which they are alike.

Figure 12 — Comparison

Contrasts may be more difficult to find because the range of intensity can vary from distinct contrasts to mild differences. Look for things which are similar in one respect and dissimilar in another. Key words to look for are "but," "nor," and "not."

Figure 13 — Contrast

In this observation exercise you will especially want to use cross-references. As you read a story or statement in the Scriptures, consider things which are similar in certain respects but different in others. Observing these contrasts will help you discern the overall truth of the Word of God.

In his letter to the Thessalonians, Paul makes two comparisons between his ministry and the role of parents with children. He compares his activities among them as being that of "a mother caring for her little children" (1 Thessalonians 2:7), and that he dealt with them "as a father deals with his own children" (2:11). Considering the characteristics of a mother, you might think about infant care, tenderness, caring for babies individually, and feeding them on schedule. Considering the role of the father, you would think of discipline, concern, instruction, and giving direction. Making these observations will give you additional insight into Paul's character and his relationship to the Thessalonians.

Several contrasts also appear in this letter. Paul stated, for example, that his preaching was "not trying to please men *but* God" (2:4). Later, as he was exhorting them, he said, "Let us not be like others who are asleep, *but* let us be alert and self-controlled" (5:6).

The Book of Hebrews frequently makes use of comparisons and contrasts. Figure 13 is a chart made from such a treatment of Christ and Aaron in Hebrews 7.

CONTRASTS BETWEEN THE TWO PRIESTHOODS
(Hebrews 7)

Chapter Divisions	MELCHIZEDEK/CHRIST	Contrasts in Verses	LEVI/AARON
7:1-3	WHO MELCHIZEDEK WAS		
7:4-10	RECEIVED TITHES FROM ABRAHAM	4	PAID TITHES TO MELCHIZEDEK THROUGH ABRAHAM
	GAVE A BLESSING	6	RECEIVED A BLESSING
	LIVES FOREVER	8	DIED
7:11-19	FREE FROM AN IMPERFECT LAW	11	MARRIED TO AN IMPERFECT LAW
	PRIESTHOOD UNCHANGED BY VIRTUE OF HIS LIFE	12/16	PRIESTHOOD CHANGED BY VIRTUE OF HIS TRIBAL HERITAGE
	COULD MAKE PEOPLE PERFECT	19	COULD NOT MAKE PEOPLE PERFECT
7:20-22	WITH AN OATH	20	WITHOUT AN OATH
7:23-25	ONE PRIEST	23/24	MANY PRIESTS
	EVER LIVETH	23/24	DEATH
	ABLE TO SAVE	25	UNABLE TO SAVE
7:26-28	SEPARATE FROM SIN	26/27	SINNER
	OFFERED HIMSELF ONCE	27	OFFERED SACRIFICES (animals) MANY TIMES
	PERFECT	28	WEAK
	GOD/MAN	28	MAN

Figure 14

Investigate the Use of Old Testament References

The only Scriptures people had in the early days of the church were the writings of the Old Testament. The advent of Jesus Christ was the fulfillment of what the Old Testament had promised. Because of this fact, New Testament writers constantly dip back into the Old Testament to show how Jesus is the Messiah or to relate the implications of this fact to the lives of people.

The Book of Galatians is a beautiful example of this. Paul, reasoning from the Old Testament, convinced those in the province of Galatia that Jesus was the Christ. Then the Judaizers followed his ministry, arguing from the same Old Testament that people coming to Christ had to follow Old Testament laws, such as circumcision, in order to be saved. In his letter, Paul argues back that the Old Testament itself teaches that these laws that the Judaizers were pressing should no longer be kept. Paul's selection and use of Old Testament references is absolutely masterful in proving this difficult point.

Note the Progression of an Idea or Thought Chain

Thought chains graphically associate similar ideas. You will need a study Bible you can mark and some colored pencils. Look through a passage for similar thoughts. Then using one color for similar ideas, draw a circle around each one. Using the same color, connect the circles with thin lines and give the chain a title. Use different colors to make other chains of associated thoughts.

Now consider chain titles to see how they fit together to make one theme for the passage. In Figure 14 only one chain has been worked out. It is the "Character of the Minister." Other chains might be titled "Effect of the Ministry" and "Concern for Young Christians." These lead to the theme, "How to Minister to Young Believers."

1 THESSALONIANS 2:1

Paul's Ministry in Thessalonica

2 You know, brothers, that our visit to you was not a failure. ²We had previously suffered and been insulted in Philippi, as you know, but with the help of our God we dared to tell you his gospel in spite of strong opposition. ³For the appeal we make does not spring from error or impure motives, nor are we trying to trick you. ⁴On the contrary, we speak as men approved by God to be entrusted with the gospel. We are not trying to please men but God, who tests our hearts. ⁵You know we never used flattery, nor did we put on a mask to cover up greed—God is our witness. ⁶We were not looking for praise from men, not from you or anyone else.

⁷As apostles of Christ we could have been a burden to you, but we were gentle among you, like a mother caring for her little children. ⁸We loved you so much that we were delighted to share with you not only the gospel of God but our lives as well, because you had become so dear to us. ⁹Surely you remember, brothers, our toil and hardship; we worked night and day in order not to be a burden to anyone while we preached the gospel of God to you.

¹⁰You are witnesses, and so is God, of how holy, righteous and blameless we were among you who believed. ¹¹For you know that we dealt with each of you as a father deals with his own children, ¹²encouraging, comforting and urging you to live lives worthy of God, who calls you into his kingdom and glory.

Figure 15

In 2 Timothy 1, Paul talks about not being ashamed of the gospel. Note his progression of thought:

- Verse 8—"Do not be ashamed . . ."
- Verse 12—"I am not ashamed . . ."
- Verse 16—"Onesiphorus . . . was not ashamed . . ."

A more technical illustration of this may be seen in the idea of *imputation* used by Paul in the Book of Romans:

- Romans 3:21-31—the imputation of Christ's righteousness to the sinner
- Romans 4—imputation illustrated in the life of Abraham
- Romans 5:12-21—the imputation of Adam's sin to mankind
- Romans 6–8—the outworking of imputation in the life of the believer

Be Alert for Proportions

The law of proportions is one of the keys to maintaining a balance of emphasis in your personal Bible study. Make sure that you are observing such proportions as importance of the subject, people involved, the time element, and the subject matter itself. The following chart of the Book of Acts will help you observe the time element as it is found in the book.

Chapters	1	2	3-8	9-12	13-14	15	16:1-18:22	18:23-21:16	21:17-28:31
Time Span	50 days	1 day	2 years	9 years	1½ years	few days	2½ years	4 years	5 years

Figure 16

Observe also how much of Paul's first letter to the Thessalonians deals with the second coming of Jesus Christ. The topic is mentioned in each chapter and discussed at length toward the end of the letter (see 1 Thessalonians 1:10; 2:19; 3:13; 4:13-18; 5:1-11). Also notice the references Paul made to his unblamable conduct and behavior before the people in Thessalonica. These proportion observations can give you a clue to Paul's major emphases in writing that first epistle.

Record Repetitions

As you do your Bible study, take particular note of the repetition of words, phrases, and expressions in the passage being studied. You can do this by making a chart of the repetitions in the passage. The benefit of this method is not in filling out the chart, but in enabling you to ask the right questions after you have seen the repetitions in the passage. An example from 1 Thessalonians 3 may be seen below in Figure 16.

WORD OR PHRASE	NUMBER OF REPETITIONS	VERSES USED
FAITH	5	2, 5, 6, 7, 10
AFFLICTION	3	3, 4, 7

Figure 17

Observing that the word *faith* appears five times in this section, you might ask, ''Why is faith mentioned so often?'' Seeing the repetition of the word *affliction,* you might conclude that faith is increased by the right response to affliction.

In almost every passage you will study, there will be words or phrases that will be repeated. Look for them and examine them carefully. Determine why they are repeated and how they are related.

Observation also includes the opposite aspect of repetition—omission. As you study a given passage, think to yourself, *What words or phrases would I have included in writing this?* Then continue your observation by asking questions like, ''If these thoughts and ideas are omitted, why are they omitted?'' ''Is there a substitute the author used?'' ''What is that substitute?'' Obviously, it is much more difficult to observe omissions than to see repetitions, but omissions must be carefully noted.

For example, a notable omission in the Book of Acts is the complete absence of the word *love.* On the other hand, the results of love, unity and oneness, are mentioned often.

Visualize the Verbs

Another key to making good observations is discerning the action or movement of a passage. In grammar, action is carried by verbs. They tell us what is being done, and reveal the movement or flow of a passage.

Underline all the verbs in the passage you are studying, then list them on your Bible study worksheet. After you have underlined them all, examine them carefully. What kind of action do the verbs portray? Are most of them active or passive? Does the subject influence the action or is it being acted on? Do the verbs indicate that the passage is basically a narrative or poetry? Are there any quotations? Are the verbs imperatives—do they give commands? Which verbs are repeated? What is the significance of their usages?

For example, in Hebrews 11 the verbs are active, indicating that the believer has a vital role in the life of faith. He must respond to what God is doing in his life.

In Ephesians 1:3-14 the verbs are passive and indicate that the believer is acted on. Observing the use of verbs in this passage gives us the clue that the emphasis is on what is done for the believer rather than what he does or must do.

The following illustration from 1 Thessalonians 1 shows the underlining process (Fig. 18).

Picture the Illustrations

Have you ever been struck by how many verbal illustrations there are in the Bible? Many of the writers God used to record His Word talked in pictures. Jesus used this device often as He called His followers vines, sheep, fishers of men, farmers, and many other such expressions.

As you study, pay particular attention to finding illustrations being used by the writer of the passage you are observing. Some illustrations are obvious, like the vine and the branches in John 15. Others are not so obvious, but Scripture abounds in illustrations

1 Thessalonians

1 Paul, Silas[a] and Timothy,

To the church of the Thessalonians, who are in God the Father and the Lord Jesus Christ:

Grace and peace to you.

Thanksgiving for the Thessalonians' Faith

[2]We always <u>thank</u> God for all of you, <u>mentioning</u> you in our prayers. [3]We continually <u>remember</u> before our God and Father your work produced by faith, your labor <u>prompted</u> by love, and your endurance <u>inspired</u> by hope in our Lord Jesus Christ.

[4]Brothers <u>loved</u> by God, we <u>know</u> that he has <u>chosen</u> you, [5]because our gospel <u>came</u> to you not simply with words, but also with power, with the Holy Spirit and with deep conviction. You <u>know</u> how we <u>lived</u> among you for your sake. [6]You <u>became</u> imitators of us and of the Lord; in spite of severe suffering, you <u>welcomed</u> the message with the joy <u>given</u> by the Holy Spirit. [7]And so you <u>became</u> a model to all the believers in Macedonia and Achaia. [8]The Lord's message <u>rang out</u> from you not only in Macedonia and Achaia—your faith in God <u>has become known</u> everywhere. Therefore we do not need <u>to say</u> anything about it, [9]for they themselves <u>report</u> what kind of reception you <u>gave us.</u> They <u>tell</u> how you <u>turned</u> to God from idols <u>to serve</u> the living and true God, [10]and <u>to wait</u> for his Son from heaven, whom he <u>raised</u> from the dead—Jesus, who <u>rescues</u> us from the coming wrath.

Figure 18

and word pictures. In James 3 alone, there are at least nine different illustrations (and comparisons and contrasts).

Once you observe an illustration, think through on how it clarifies the subject of the passage. Try to think of other illustrations that Scripture uses to present this subject. Then compare and contrast your illustration with these. For example, Paul's use of a thief in the night illustrates the need for being prepared (1 Thessalonians 5:2); a woman with child illustrates suddenness (5:3); and a breastplate of faith illustrates being equipped (5:8).

If there are no illustrations in the passage you are studying, which is highly unlikely, then look for illustrations and examples in other portions of Scripture relevant to the passage under study.

Examine the Explanations

An explanation is anything that is used to illustrate, clarify, illuminate, describe, or demonstrate. An explanation may be one verse long or a whole chapter.

To understand an explanation clearly, you must follow the logic of the writer. What point is he trying to make? How is he trying to make it? How does he present it?

Sometimes the Scriptures explain a question that is not stated but implied. Often a statement in one verse will cause you to ask a question, and the following verse will then answer your question. Be sure to note this kind of tie-in between verses and paragraphs.

For example, Paul said, "We maintain that a man is justified by faith apart from observing the law" (Romans 3:28). A natural question which may come out of observation on this statement might be, "Could people in the Old Testament be saved?"

In the next two paragraphs (Romans 4:1-8), Paul explains how Abraham and David were both justified by faith without the deeds of the law. This helps explain the earlier statement, but don't presume that the paragraphs of Romans 4 were written primarily to explain your question on Romans 3:28.

Be Sensitive to Connecting Words and Conjunctions

Someone once said that the little two-letter word *if* connotes the difference between law and grace. It certainly connotes condition, and when speaking of what God wants to do in the lives of people is an immediate indication of whether the people's response will affect what God promises to do. For example, God said to the nation of Israel, "Now if you obey me fully and keep my covenant, then out of all nations you will be my treasured possession" (Exodus 19:5). This did not come about because Israel did not obey.

Other important connectives include *therefore,* which introduces a summary of ideas or the results of some action; *because, or, for,* and *then* are words that often introduce a reason or result; *but* lets you know there is a contrast that follows; and *in order that* is a phrase often used to set forth a purpose. Stay alert for these in your study.

Be Willing to Change Your Viewpoint

In order to change your viewpoint, you will have to eliminate preconceived ideas. Do not allow these to control or even color your thinking about the Word of God. Read your study passage as though you were an impartial observer. In his first letter to the Thessalonians, Paul levels several accusations at a particular group of people (1 Thessalonians 2:14-16). At first glance, out of some preconceived ideas you might have, you might envision these people as being vicious and cruel. But the fact is that this group was well respected and well thought of in their society. With this in mind, you may need to change your viewpoint and reread this passage making new observations.

One of the more interesting ways to change your viewpoint is to put yourself in another person's shoes. How would you feel if you were the author of this epistle? (When Paul wrote Ephesians, he was in prison.) How would you as a recipient understand the message? (Paul rebukes his recipients in 1 Corinthians.) What would a third party at the scene think of the situation as he listened to Paul? (Silas and Timothy were with Paul when he wrote 1 Thessalonians.) What would strict Jews think of Paul's letter to the Galatians? Or strict Romans of James' letter? You need to learn to observe from different perspectives.

Mark Your Bible as You Read

You should have a study Bible with wide margins that you can use to record your observations. (Many are available on the market today—check with your local bookstore or the American Bible Society.) As you make observations on a passage you have chosen to study, mark it in the text and in the margins. You may use some or all of the following devices: brackets, parallel diagonal lines in the margin, circles, vertical lines in the margins, arrows, inked in words and/or phrases, marked through words and/or phrases, underlining (see the section *Visualizing the Verbs* earlier in the chapter). Also you may create your own symbols, marks, and system.

In marking a study Bible (not a good reading Bible made of India paper) you can use pen and ink, ballpoint, and fine and course felt-tip pens. To mark *through* words and phrases for emphasis use a light highlighter felt-tip pen to allow you to read the words through it. Use india ink in marking a fine Bible. Some examples follow in a marked-up copy of 1 Thessalonians 2:1-12. (Fig. 19.)

Summary

Do not become discouraged if your observations do not immediately bear the fruit you desire. It is hard work and, like any other skill, takes time to develop. Nor should you feel like a failure if you are unable to apply all these suggestions to your Bible study. They have been given to serve as a set of "handles" for you to get a grip on *observation*. Some of these "handles" won't apply to every passage.

---

1 THESSALONIANS 2:1

Paul's Ministry in Thessalonica

2 You <u>know</u>, brothers, that our visit to you was not a failure. We had previously suffered and been insulted in Philippi as you know, but with the help of our God we dared to tell you <u>his gospel</u> in spite of strong opposition. ³For the appeal we make does not spring from error or impure motives, nor are we trying to trick you. ⁴On the contrary, we speak as men approved by God to be entrusted with <u>the</u> gospel. We are not trying to please men but God, who tests <u>our hearts</u>. ⁵You know we never used flattery, nor did we put on a mask to cover up greed—God is our witness. ⁶We were not looking for praise from men, not from you or anyone else.

⁷As apostles of Christ we could have been a burden to you, but we were gentle among you, (like a mother) caring for her little children. ⁸We loved you so much that we were delighted to share with you not only the <u>gospel of God</u> but our lives as well, because you had become so dear to us. ⁹Surely you remember, brothers, our toil and hardship; we worked night and day in order not to be a burden to anyone while we preached the <u>gospel of God</u> to you.

¹⁰You are witnesses, and so is God, of how **holy, righteous and blameless we were among you** who believed. ¹¹For you know that we dealt with each of you (as a father) deals with his own children, ¹²<u>encouraging</u>, <u>comforting</u> and <u>urging</u> you to <u>live</u> lives worthy of God, who <u>calls</u> you into his kingdom and glory.

See Acts 16

Contrast

←

Key: Sharing our lives with others

←

Figure 19

You will find prayerful reflection to be indispensable. Be imaginative. Put yourself in the role of the writer or the people you are studying. How did they respond? How should they have responded? Seek to feel things as they must have felt them. Dialogue with them.

Also, be patient. If, after your study, you find you have overlooked an important *observation,* remember that others never stop discovering new and fresh insights from passages with which they have lived for many years.

14 Interpretation: The Role of a Decision Maker

INTERPRETATION

Understanding the meaning of what has been observed in Bible study.

Observation seeks to answer the question "What does it *say?*" Interpretation seeks to answer the question "What does it *mean?*" The dictionary defines interpretation as "The act or process of explaining; to clarify the meaning of; to offer an explanation." In this part of the Bible study, you are seeking to clarify the *meaning* of the passage and understand the writer's *meaning* as he communicated these words to the people of his day.

Foundational to this step in Bible study is the application of the 24 rules of interpretation stated and explained in the first section of this book. They form the ground rules for understanding the Bible. You should review them periodically, for the value of your Bible study will be in direct proportion to their application.

Interpretation follows observation. It is analogous to drawing the net around a school of fish you have just caught. It is an exciting part of your Bible study, for it is a time in which you come to some conclusions. The individual insights that made up your observations are now brought together into a coherent whole.

The three parts to the interpretive process are purpose, key thought, and flow.

Purpose

Here your objective is to determine why the writer is bringing up the subject. Paul, writing to the church at Rome, said, "For everything that was written in the past was written to teach us" (Romans 15:4). What the Holy Spirit has included in the Bible is there in order that we might learn from it. Determining the *purpose* of the book, passage, poem, story, or whatever else is the first step in interpretation.

As you do a synthetic study of Galatians, for example, you learn that Paul's purpose for writing that letter was to communicate that a person is justified by faith in Jesus Christ apart from the works of the law.

Sometimes the purpose is fairly easy to discover, as is the case with the Gospel of John. John states his purpose for writing: "These are written that you may believe that Jesus is the Christ [the Old Testament Messiah], the Son of God, and that by believing you may have life in his name" (John 20:31).

The purpose of the writer of Hebrews beginning with a comparison of Jesus Christ to angels (Chapters 1–2) is to establish the fact that God's revelation to man in the person of Christ is through no mere angel. Rather, He is the eternal Creator God of the universe.

In the Old Testament, when God wanted to speak authoritatively to His people, He frequently sent an angel. Jesus is infinitely better than the angels.

As you study the narration of an event, seek to discover its purpose. Why did Elijah retreat into the wilderness after his spectacular victory at Mount Carmel? (See 1 Kings 18–19.) Why did God keep Israel at Mount Sinai for such a long time after the Exodus? (See Exodus 19–40.) Similar questions should be asked in your study of Bible topics and biographies.

Key Thought

The *key thought* is the "big idea," theme, or distilled essence of the book, passage, topic, or person you are studying. As much as possible, state the key thought in one sentence. Make it a complete sentence with a subject and predicate. Generally speaking, the longer and more complicated the theme, the less you understand what it is. A good rule of thumb is to try to limit your key thought to about 20-30 words. The purpose of the theme is to state the main truth or spiritual principle as clearly and as succinctly as possible. Generally there is only one theme to a passage, not many. It may be stated in different ways, but the core should remain the same.

A possible theme for 1 Peter 2 might be stated as follows: "The believer is called to follow the example of the rejected Christ into a life of submission and suffering at the hands of a hostile world."

In a study of the life of Rahab and why she was considered great in God's sight, the theme might be stated as follows: "The reason for Rahab's inclusion in God's Hall of Fame [Hebrews 11] is found in her willingness to take great risks for God on the basis of little knowledge."

Or let us say you are studying the training of the 12 disciples in the years of Jesus' public ministry. What was the *main* thing Jesus sought to impart to them? Your topical study would reveal that the "big idea" Jesus sought to communicate was *faith*. The articulation of your key thought would center around this idea of faith.

If a group was doing a study on what Jesus sought to impart to the disciples, all should conclude that faith was the main truth, though the wording of that truth might vary from person to person.

Flow

How did the writer get to where he is? How did he arrive at the theme? Determining the flow is the third step in the process of interpretation. It is the movement of the argument, narrative, or teaching. In a topical study the flow is expressed in the natural unfolding of the topic.

Maybe you decide to study the topic of *prayer*. Because it is such a large topic you elect to narrow it to what the Gospel of John teaches about it. The flow is answered in such questions as: "How does John handle the subject of prayer?" "Is it by teaching, example, or combination?" "Through whose life or lives is it seen?"

In another area, you might ask: "How does Jesus go about teaching His disciples faith?" "Is there any pattern?" "Does He combine teaching and experience?"

These three aspects of interpretation, *purpose, key thought*, and *flow* are seen in each of the types of Bible study. It is at the same time both an interesting and an important part of your study. Attack it in a spirit of expectation.

15 Correlation: The Role of a Coordinator

CORRELATION

Relating what is being studied with other portions of Scriptures and within the section itself.

One dictionary defines *correlation* as: "To bring two or more things into relation with one another; the act of relating." This is an exciting and highly rewarding aspect of Bible study. In scope it will range from relating one verse to another, to relating one paragraph to another, and to relating the various chapters of a book to one another.

Since the Bible is truth, and all truth due to its divine origin is unified, it is important to relate various

189

truths to one another. It makes the Scriptures coherent and helps the student to be consistent with what the rest of the Bible says on any given subject.

Some basic ways of correlating your study are through cross-references, paraphrases, outlines, and charts.

Cross-references

This expression of correlation is to compare a word, verse, idea, event, or story with another portion of Scripture. Often the content of one passage will help clarify the content of another. At times you will want to cross-reference the thought with another thought found within the passage you are studying. At other times you will look for the cross-reference outside the passage, but within the book. Then too, there will be times when you will want to go outside the book you are studying into another portion of the Bible.

Several types of cross-references are available for your use.

Word cross-references—At times in your study you will discover an important word that you may want to cross reference. It may appear important to the passage and you may want to investigate it further. The person Melchizedek is such an example (Hebrews 5:6). Cross-referencing from within Hebrews, you find him discussed at some length in Chapter 7. Outside of Hebrews, he is introduced in Genesis 14:18 and briefly mentioned in Psalm 110:4.

This kind of cross-reference becomes strategically important in your topical and biographical studies.

Parallel cross-references—These are verses or thoughts that say virtually the same thing. Often the wording and context are slightly different, giving you fresh insight on the subject you are studying. The Gospels and some of Paul's epistles are places where this type of cross-reference is readily used. Paul wrote to the Ephesians, "Speak to one another with psalms, hymns, and spiritual songs. Sing and make music in your heart to the Lord" (Ephesians 5:19). You may cross reference that with his exhortation to the Colossians: "Let the word of Christ dwell in you richly as you teach and counsel one another with all wisdom, and as you sing psalms, hymns and spiritual songs with gratitude in your hearts to God" (Colossians 3:16). Comparing the context of these two statements is a fascinating study in and of itself. The parable of the sower in Matthew 13:3-23 may be cross referenced with the parallel accounts in Mark 4:3-20 and Luke 8:4-15.

Corresponding cross-references—The New Testament writers frequently quote from the Old Testament. A study of the context of the passage quoted is often helpful in understanding the point the author is making. When Jesus was in Nazareth, the town in which He was raised, He read from the Scroll of Isaiah in the local synagogue (see Luke 4:16-30). When you cross reference Luke 4:18 with Isaiah 61:1-2, you note that Jesus ends His quotation of Isaiah *halfway* through verse 2. Why does He do this? He does this because the Isaiah passage includes both of His comings—the first in humility and the second in glory—and He was at that time in Nazareth only in His first advent.

Another type of corresponding cross-reference is where another portion of Scripture refers to the same event. For example, Paul said, "You know, brothers, that our visit to you was not a failure" (1 Thessalonians 2:1). When did this occur? Luke tells in the Book of Acts (see Acts 17:1-10).

Idea cross-references—These are the most helpful cross-references in the analytical study. Here you endeavor to capture the thought of the author in the verse or paragraph being studied and compare it with a similar thought elsewhere in the Bible. The key thought of 1 Peter 1:23, for example, is that a person needs to be born again by the eternal Word of God. When cross referenced with John 3:1-8, you find Jesus saying that a person needs to be born again, but by the Holy Spirit. Why the difference? That is, why does Peter say it is by the Word and Jesus by the Spirit? Because you cannot know the living God apart from the Bible and you cannot know the Bible apart from the Spirit of the living God. The two are inseparable, and for this reason may be interchanged (see also Hebrews 4:12-13).

Contrasting cross-references—Contrasting examples in the Bible help you pinpoint proper action as well as bringing into balance a proper understanding of what the Bible teaches on a subject. Perhaps it will be helpful to illustrate both.

Contrast how Jesus handled temptation in Matthew 4 at the beginning of His ministry with how Adam handled it in Genesis 3. The "first Adam" met Satan and was defeated; the "second Adam" met Satan and was victorious.

In Paul's first letter to the Corinthians he makes an interesting comment. "I say this as a concession, not as a command" (1 Corinthians 7:6). Some may conclude that what follows was Paul's idea, and not from the Lord. A contrasting cross-reference brings important balance to this statement. Paul had previously told them, "This is what we speak, not in words taught us by human wisdom but in words taught by the Spirit, expressing spiritual truths in spiritual words" (1 Corinthians 2:13). Here Paul reminds us that even that which is spoken by "concession" is what the Holy Spirit is teaching.

A number of good sources of cross-references are available to you today. If you are cross-referencing a word, use a good concordance such as *Strong's Exhaustive Concordance of the Bible* or *Young's Analytical Concordance to the Bible*. Many Bibles have excellent lists of cross-references in the margins next to the verses or in an abbreviated concordance in the back of the Bible. *The Treasury of Scripture Knowledge* is probably the best source of cross-references. It lists 500,000 difficult cross-references and includes every book in the Bible.

Don't fall into the trap of relying completely on these helps rather than thinking for yourself. Often cross-references that give you the most satisfaction are those you will have thought of yourself.

Personal Paraphrase

Another form of correlation is the paraphrase—stating the content of the section you are studying in contemporary language by relating it to itself. Some modern paraphrases provide good examples of this form of correlation. The following excerpts are from *The New Testament in Modern English, Revised Edition* by J. B. Phillips and *The Living Bible* by Kenneth Taylor.

---

1 Thessalonians 2:7-8 (PH)	**1 Thessalonians 2:7-8** (LB)
"Our attitude among you was one of tenderness, rather like a nurse caring for her babies. Because we loved you, it was a joy to us to give you not only the Gospel of God but our very hearts—so dear had you become to us."	"But we were gentle among you as a mother feeding and caring for her own children. We loved you dearly—so dearly that we gave you not only God's message, but our own lives too."

Figure 20

Scripture Versions

When you are being creative in your personal paraphrasing, do not stray from the basic content of the passage you are studying. Your paraphrase must express the thought of the writer, though in different words.

Detailed Outline

Some people enjoy using a detailed outline for their correlation of a passage within itself. This type of outline includes every idea mentioned in the section you are studying without omitting any details. Such an outline of 1 Thessalonians 1:1-5 appears in Figure 20.

I. PAUL'S GREETING (1:1)

A. From: Paul, Silvanus, and Timothy

B. To: The Church of the Thessalonians – in God and Christ

C. Greeting: Grace to you and peace

II. PAUL'S PRAYER AND GOSPEL MINISTRY (1:2-5)

A. Paul's prayer for the Thessalonians (vv. 2,3)
   1. Always giving thanks for them
   2. Constantly remembering their:
      a. Work of faith   } in Christ
      b. Labor of love   in the presence of God
      c. Steadfastness of hope }

B. Paul's Gospel Ministry to the Thessalonians (vv. 4-5)
   1. God loved the Thessalonians and chose them
   2. The Gospel came:
      a. In Word
      b. In Power
      c. In the Holy Spirit
      d. With full conviction
   3. Paul's manner of living was for their sake

Figure 21

Charts

This method of correlation maximizes your opportunity to be creative in your Bible study. For this reason it is for many the most fun and rewarding. The chart is also one of the most effective ways of grasping the unity of a passage, book, or topic. Its purpose is to give you a "bird's eye" view of the principal thoughts, so you can relate them to one another.

The chart is simply one of the many possible tools you may want to use in Bible study. It is not a substitute for your outline or other forms of examination; it can be a helpful augmentation. In fact, your chart will utilize your outline and will be one of the last things you do.

A variety of ways may be used to make a chart. Your selection of the type will depend on what you are trying to accomplish.

Horizontal Charts

These charts are most helpful in seeing the whole of your study of a passage or book, in comparing various elements in your study, and in making a topical grid. They are versatile, allowing for many possibilities of development and do not follow any rigid rules. Use your creativity and draw them in such a way that they will serve you.

SURVEY CHARTS—These charts enable you to see the whole of your study at one glance, whether it be a passage or a whole book. Take a sheet of paper (8½'' x 11'' is a good size) and draw a line the long way down the middle. Divide that line according to the number of sections in your study outline. Place your titles (of the outline) in the upper section with the references, and note the correlations in the lower section. Remember, you are trying to relate the parts to the whole visually. Keep the chart neat and orderly, but be creative. You can draw these charts on passages (chapters) and whole books, small or large.

The simplest survey chart is on a chapter, as illustrated in Figure 21. Each section on the chart contains a paragraph and the divisions are indicated by the verse numbers in the corners. Write your paragraph titles at the top of each section, then list the key thoughts that led you to those titles under them; you may want to tie related thoughts together with arrows. Finally, record your con-

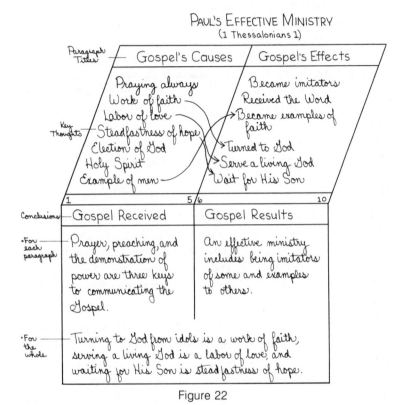

Figure 22

clusions—for each paragraph and for the whole passage—in the bottom section of the chart. Figure 22 is another variety of a survey chart on a chapter—2 Timothy 2.

Survey charts of whole books may also vary in complexity. Figure 23 illustrates a simple chart of the Epistle to the Ephesians; Figure 24 shows more details on the Book of 1 Peter; and Figure 25 is a very detailed chart on the Epistle to the Hebrews.

CALL TO COMMITMENT
2 TIMOTHY 2

HARDSHIP/PERSECUTION SUFFERING ——⌃ ——————⌃ APOSTASY

FAITHFUL MEN INVESTING IN NEEDY PEOPLE

	1		7	8		13	14		19	20		26
	FAITHFUL MEN			FAITHFUL CHRIST			FAITHFUL WORD			FAITHFUL SERVANT		
	COMMIT			COMMITMENT			CONCENTRATE			CONSECRATE		
	TIMOTHY			PAUL								
	MEN			MESSAGE			MINISTRY			MATURITY		
	ENTRUST			ENDURE			EQUIP			EXCELLENCE		
	FAITHFULNESS						UNFAITHFULNESS					
	GRACE						GRACIOUSNESS					

Commitment to a Vision

Commitment to Christ

Commitment to Truth

Commitment to Character

Figure 23

THE EPISTLE TO THE EPHESIANS

	PREDETERMINED PURPOSE	PRAYER FOR UNDERSTANDING	PURPOSE APPROPRIATED	PRAYER FOR APPLICATION	PERSONAL RESPONSIBILITIES	PRAYER
	1:1-14	1:15-23	2:1—3:13	3:14-21	4:1—6:18	6:19-20
	DOCTRINE				APPLICATION	
	POSITION				RESPONSIBILITY	
	PASSIVE				ACTIVE	
	WHAT CHRIST DID				WHAT WE DO	
	CHURCH'S HEAVENLY POSITION				CHURCH'S EARTHLY CHALLENGE	
	INDIVIDUAL				CORPORATE	
	GOD'S ACTIONS				OUR PROPOSED REACTIONS	
	EXPLANATION OF POSITION				EXHORTATION TO LIVE	

Figure 24

1 PETER
"SYLLABUS FOR SUFFERING SAINTS"
"HOW TO HOLD UP, NOT FOLD UP"

GRACE AND PEACE

SALVATION	SUBMISSION	SUFFERING
Introduction (1:1-2) Plot Permanent vs. Passing	Introduction (2:11-12)	Conclusion (5:12-14)
THE PRIVILEGES OF SALVATION (1:3-12)	IN THE STATE (2:13-17) **CIVIL**	AS A CITIZEN (3:13-4:6)
THE PRODUCTS OF SALVATION (1:13-25)	IN THE HOUSEHOLD (2:18-25) **SOCIAL**	AS A SAINT (4:7-19)
THE PROCESS OF SALVATION (2:1-10)	IN THE FAMILY (3:1-7) **DOMESTIC**	AS A SHEPHERD (5:1-7)
	Summary (3:8-12)	AS A SOLDIER (5:8-11)
DOCTRINE IS DYNAMIC!	THE CHRISTIAN'S LIFE-STYLE!	THE CHISEL TO SHAPE THE SOUL!

1:3	2:10	2:11	3:12	3:13	5:11

THE DESTINY OF THE CHRISTIAN	THE DUTY OF THE CHRISTIAN	THE DISCIPLINE OF THE CHRISTIAN
Our Relationship to God	Our Relationship to Others	Our Relationship to Circumstances
Our Belief	Our Behavior	Our Buffeting
Our Relationship	Our Responsibility	Our Rejoicing

GRACE AND PEACE

Figure 25

THE EPISTLE TO THE HEBREWS
A COMPARISON OF CHRIST TO THE OLD TESTAMENT
CHRIST: THE FULFILLMENT OF OLD TESTAMENT MESSIANIC PROMISES

CHRIST THE PERFECT HIGH PRIEST

HE IS BETTER . . .

	than Angels	than Moses	than Aaron	Assurance	Priesthood	Covenant	Sacrifice
	THE PERSON AND WORK OF CHRIST	THE POSITION OF CHRIST	THE PROVISION OF CHRIST	THE PERFECT PRIESTHOOD OF CHRIST	THE PROMISES OF CHRIST	THE PERFECTION OF CHRIST	THE PLACE OF CHRIST'S MINISTRY	THE PRIESTLY MINISTRY OF CHRIST
	1:1-14	2:1-18	3:1-19	4:1-16	5:1-14	6:1-20	7:1-28	8:1-13	9:1—10:18
	Created the Universe	Redeemed Men	Built the Church	Provided Acceptance	Demonstrated Obedience	Provided a Hope	Intercedes Continuously	Established a Covenant of Grace	Sacrificed Himself

Heed the Word of God 2:1-4
Don't Be Hardened in Unbelief 3:12-14
Maturity Affects Assurance 5:11—6:12

WARNINGS

Preeminence of Christ
Preeminence of Christ's Priesthood

What Have We? — We have such a High Priest

INSTRUCTION

A NEW COVENANT

SUPERIOR PERSON — SUPERIOR MINISTRY

What Christ Did — His Person

CHRIST THE PERFECT WAY

A BETTER FAITH . . .

ENDURANCE OF FAITH	EXPLANATION AND EXAMPLES OF FAITH	ENCUMBRANCES OF FAITH	EXPRESSIONS OF FAITH
10:19-39	11:1-40	12:1-29	13:1-25
Provided a New and Living Way	Gave Promises	Is by Our Side	Is the Same Always

Don't Reject Christ 10:26-31
Heed the Word of God 12:25-29

Practical Teaching and Exhortation

Having, therefore, let us . . .

EXHORTATION

AN OLD FAITH

SUPERIOR LIFE

What We Do — Our Response

Figure 26

COMPARATIVE CHARTS—These charts are used to sort out a mixture of information for the purpose of comparison and contrast. To make your chart, take a sheet of paper (8½" x 11" preferably) and divide it into the desired number of squares. Horizontally state the things to be compared; vertically state the people or events. Figure 27 illustrates this type of chart by comparing the journeys of the Apostle Paul, while Figure 28 charts his imprisonments. (These two charts are not filled in—you can do that sometime— but illustrate the concept.)

A TOPICAL GRID—Many passages of Scripture deal with one particular topic. For example, 1 Corinthians 13 is about love, 1 Corinthians 15 about the resurrection, and 2 Peter 2 about false teachers. The themes of these chapters are usually best stated in a word or phrase, rather than a sentence. Figure 26 illustrates a topical grid on 2 Thessalonians 2.

TOPIC: FOLLOW-UP   CHAPTER: 2 THESSALONIANS 2

Verse	Positive Characteristics	Negative Attitudes	Relationships	Activities
4	approved by God; entrusted with Gospel	not speaking to please men		
5		no flattering speech; not greedy.		
6		no glory seeking; not asserting authority		
7	gentle		a nursing mother	caring for them
8	having fond affection; very dear to them			imparting lives

Figure 27

PAUL'S JOURNEYS

Journeys	Scripture	Dates	Places Visited and Length of Stay	Churches Established and the Date	Men Traveling with Paul	Letters Written and Dates
1						
2						
3						

Figure 28

PAUL'S IMPRISONMENTS

Imprisonments	Scripture	Dates	Men Paul Appeared Before	Reason for Imprisonment	Men Sent out by Paul and Where Sent	Men with Paul	Letters Written and Dates
Caesarean							
First Roman							
Second Roman							

Figure 29

In the left hand column list the references that will break the chapter up into smaller portions. The smaller portions may be paragraphs, sentences, or individual verses.

Next, determine what you want to investigate about this topic and list these categories horizontally. Some of them are illustrated in Figure 26. This type of chart will correlate the whole chapter for you.

Vertical Charts

These charts also may be used in different ways: to correlate the content of a chapter or section of a book, to compare and contrast people and events, and to sort out chronological events. Again, you should use your creativity to draw them in such ways that they will be most useful to you.

PASSAGE DESCRIPTION—To correlate the content of a chapter or passage, first divide the chapter you are studying into paragraphs. Mark down the beginning verse and the ending verse of each paragraph on your chart. For example, in 1 Thessalonians 1 you will find two paragraphs, verses 1-5 and verses 6-10.

1 THESSALONIANS 1	
PARAGRAPH 1 — vv. 1-5 v. 1	PARAGRAPH 2 — vv. 6-10 v. 6
v. 5	v. 10

Figure 30

The next step is to write in key thoughts from the paragraph in the block allotted to it. Avoid interpretation at this point; just record what you observe.

1 THESSALONIANS 1	

PARAGRAPH 1 — vv. 1-5
v. 1 — Paul greets the
         Thessalonians
     — Paul prays
     — Paul brought the
         Gospel to them
 	
v. 5
	PARAGRAPH 2 — vv. 6-10
	v. 6 — The Thessalonians . . .
	     — became imitators
	     — became examples
	     — spread their faith abroad
	     — turned to God
	
	v. 10

Figure 31

The third step is to title your paragraphs. Consider the key thoughts you have written in your chart rather than rereading the biblical text. After you have considered what you wrote for the first paragraph of 1 Thessalonians 1, you might title it, "The Gospel Received." Other possibilities might be "Paul's Ministry" or "The Enlivening Message."

1 THESSALONIANS 1	
THE GOSPEL RECEIVED	**THE GOSPEL RESULTS**

PARAGRAPH 1 — vv. 1-5
v. 1 — Paul greets the
         Thessalonians
     — Paul prays
     — Paul brought the
         Gospel to them
 	
v. 5
	PARAGRAPH 2 — vv. 6-10
	v. 6 — The Thessalonians . . .
	     — became imitators
	     — became examples
	     — spread their faith abroad
	     — turned to God
	
	v. 10

Figure 32

COMPARATIVE CHART—A vertical chart may be used to make comparisons and contrasts. Figure 13 in Chapter 13 is an illustration of this as the ministry of Christ was contrasted with that of Aaron.

CHRONOLOGICAL CHART—This type of chart is particularly helpful in sorting out chronological events in various periods of Bible history. If you, like many, have difficulty following the sequence of events in Israel's history during the period of the divided kingdom, a chart might help you understand those times. After the reign of Solomon (1 Kings 12), Israel was divided into the southern kingdom (Judah) and the northern kingdom (Israel). The division occurred about 931 B.C. The northern kingdom of Israel ended with its deportation at the hands of Assyria in 722 B.C. while Judah ended in 586 B.C. with the Babylonian captivity.

To chart the chronology of this period, place the dates vertically, with 931 at the top of the page, working down through 586 (it may take more than one sheet of paper). Horizontally place the information you want to correlate. Write in the kings of Judah and Israel, the number of years they reigned, their character (whether good or bad), and the active prophet(s) during their reign. Figure 32, a partial chart of the period, includes those elements and shows you how it may be drawn. You may also add other elements, such as, the relationship of each king to his predecessor, how each king died, and the Scripture references. You can add or delete as you want.

Pyramid Charts

This type of chart is useful in arranging your material to show movement from the specific to the general and vice versa.

Peter opens his first letter with these words: ''Praise be to the God and Father of our Lord Jesus Christ! In his great mercy he has given us new birth into a living hope through the resurrection of Jesus Christ from the dead, and into an inheritance that can never perish, spoil or fade—kept in heaven for you'' (1 Peter 1:3-4). The progression of his thought is charted in Figure 33.

PERIOD OF THE DIVIDED KINGDOM

DATE	JUDAH		YRS REIGN	GOOD/BAD	ISRAEL		YRS REIGN	GOOD/BAD	PROPHET
931	Rehoboam	931	17	bad	Jeroboam	931	22	bad	
925									
920									
915	Abijam	913	3	bad					
910	Asa	911	41	good	Nadab	910	2	bad	
905					Baasha	909	24	bad	
900									
895									
890					Elah	886	2	bad	
885					Zimri	885	7 days	bad	
880					Omri	885	12	bad	
875	Jehoshaphat	873	25	good	Ahab	874	22	bad	
870									
865									
860									
855	Jehoram	853	8	bad	Ahaziah	853	2	bad	
850					Jehoram	852	12	bad	
845	Ahaziah	841	1	bad					
840	Athaliah	841	6	bad	Jehu	841	28	bad	
835	Joash	835	40	good					
830									
825									
820									
815					Jehoahaz	814	17	bad	
810									
805									
800									
795	Amaziah	796	29	good	Jehoash	798	16	bad	

Figure 33

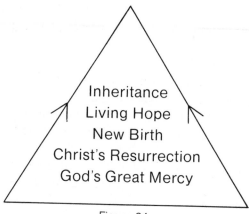

Figure 34

The whole book of 1 Peter has four major themes: sanctification, suffering, salvation, and submission. The Holy Spirit is sanctifying the believer, which builds a contrast between him and the life style of the non-Christian. The unbeliever's reaction is to persecute the Christian. The Christian's response of submission brings about the salvation of the non-Christian. You can chart all that in the manner of Figure 34.

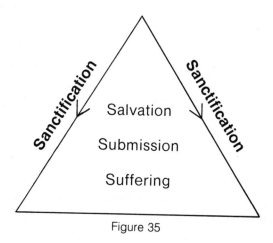

Figure 35

Whenever you have a progression of thought that flows from the general to the specific, this type of chart can be used effectively.

Illustrative Charts

This method of charting is the most creative of all the methods and also the most difficult to describe or explain. You are familiar with the proverb, "A picture is worth a thousand words." In this type of charting, you seek to draw the truths together in picture form.

Paul pictures God as being sufficient to meet all our needs (Philippians 4:13, 19). One possible way of illustrating this is shown in Figure 35.

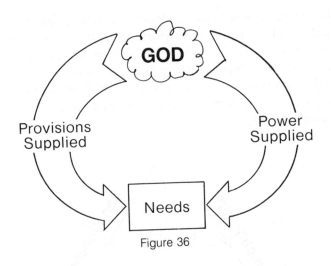

Figure 36

Romans 6–8 details the believer's freedom from the penalty, power, and presence of sin. An example of how this may be charted is found in Figure 36.

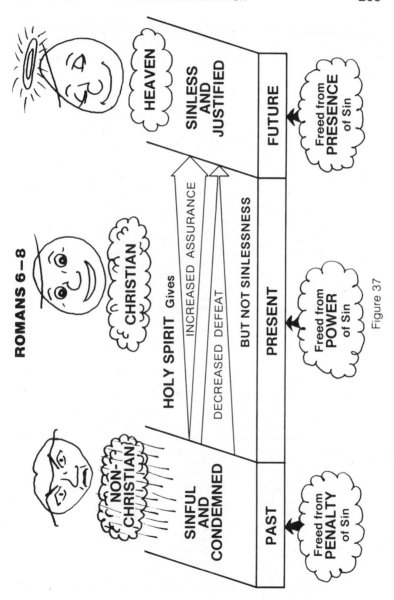

Figure 37

You can incorporate many creative approaches into your study as long as you include the content of the passage under study. Two examples of illustrative charts from 1 Thessalonians 1 are shown in Figures 37 and 38.

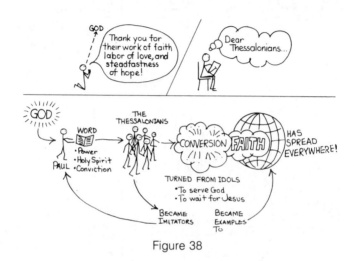

Figure 38

The Macedonian Herald

FINAL EDITION   1 DENARIUS

Thessalonica (U.P.)–Word today reached Macedonia concerning a mysterious happening in Thessalonica. After the arrival of an itinerant preacher by the name of Paul, the Thessalonians are exhibiting strange behavior. They have turned from idols to "serve God" and to wait for His Son" to return from Heaven. "God's Son," known by the name of Jesus, was reported several years ago to have been raised from death. He is also said to have power to deliver people from the "judgment" which is to come.

The message preached by Paul seems to have been accompanied by power and full conviction, for there is no other way to explain the response of the Thessalonians.

Paul has left Thessalonica, but it is reported that he continues to pray for the Thessalonians, remembering their work of faith, labor of love, and steadfastness of hope.

Figure 39

Combination Charts

At times you will want to combine the various methods of charting. Figure 39 is a chart giving an overview of Hebrews 7. It combines the *horizontal* and *illustrative* methods. Another is shown in Figure 40, in which the *horizontal* and *vertical* elements are combined.

Summary

The need to be creative in this aspect of Bible study cannot be overemphasized. So experiment. Try all kinds of things, combining what you have learned here with some of your own ideas. Use colored pens for contrast and keeping track of the movement of your ideas. Remember, your objective is to correlate the various truths in your study to one another, and in so relating them to discover new truth. Don't be intimidated by the newness of the approach or the variety of methods. Start with a portion you can handle, and go from there.

Let your creative instincts take over. Remember, the methodology is to help *you* get a grasp on the passage under study.

THE PERFECTION OF CHRIST
HIS IS A BETTER PRIESTHOOD
Hebrews 7:1-28

HIS PERSON		HIS PROMISE		HIS PERFORMANCE	
Credentials of Melchizedek	Consideration of His Greatness	Change Needed in the Old Order	Covenant Established by an Oath	Contrasting Abilities in the Priesthoods	Christ's Sacrifice of Himself
7:1-3	7:4-10	7:11-19	7:20-22	7:23-25	7:26-28
BETTER ORDER		BETTER COVENANT		BETTER PRIEST	
WHO HE WAS		WHY HE CAME		WHAT HE DID	
BECAUSE HE IS FROM MELCHIZEDEK		HE IS NOT LIMITED BY SINAI		HE IS NOT LIMITED BY THE ALTAR	

Figure 40

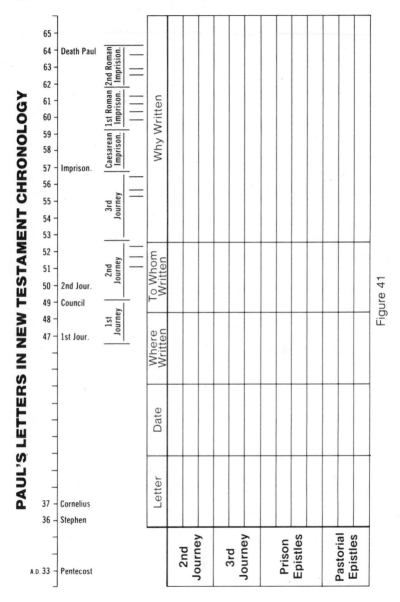

Figure 41

16 Application: The Role of an Implementor

Throughout the centuries, the application of God's Word constantly expresses itself as *the* major need in Christianity. Even in Bible times God again and again rebuked His people for failure to make application of His truths. James put it this way: ''Do not merely listen to the Word, and so deceive yourselves. Do what it says'' (James 1:22).

Learning is far easier than applying. If you find this to be true in your own life, you are no different than most Christians. Yet God

215

insists on your working at applying His truths to your life.

Rule Six under the principles of interpretation (page 33) states, "The primary purpose of the Bible is to change our lives, not increase our knowledge." In this part of your Bible study program you are prayerfully endeavoring to bring your life more completely into conformity with God's standards.

In making a personal application it is important to distinguish between emotion and volition. Often applying God's Word is an emotional experience. However, *action* and not just feeling is what God wants. Jesus' parable of the two sons makes this point quite clear (see Matthew 21:28-32). The father asked the first son to work in the vineyard, but he refused to go. Later he changed his mind and obeyed his father. The second son readily agreed to go when asked, but never showed up for work. "Which of the two did what his father wanted?" was the question Jesus asked (Matthew 21:31). You would agree that it was the first. Ideally the Lord wants both your emotions and volition, but it is when you *do* what God wants that you make application.

Procedure for Making Applications

The following seven steps are a helpful mechanical procedure for making applications.

1. *Use the Principle of Observation.* Include in your observation section of Bible study "possible" points of application as you discover them. (These have been illustrated in each of the observation sections of the five methods of Bible study.) Mark them with a colored pen or put (A) in the margin so you can identify them. List as many possible applications as you can, for you will find that every passage is "loaded" with them. Ask the Holy Spirit to help you dig them out. InterVarsity Press, in their little booklet titled *Quiet Time*, offers six suggestions—all in the form of questions—that are helpful in stimulating your mind as to possible applications. They are:

- Is there any example for me to follow?
- Is there any command for me to obey?
- Is there any error for me to avoid?
- Is there any sin for me to forsake?
- Is there any promise for me to claim?
- Is there any new thought about God Himself?

2. *Follow the Rules of Interpretation.* A proper application can only be made after you have correctly interpreted the passage. This principle is elaborated on in Rule Six, Corollary 2 (page 36). There may be many applications of a passage, but only one correct interpretation.

Remember too, a literal interpretation is always best unless the text demands otherwise. Rule Ten (page 49) may be reviewed for an elaboration of this point.

3. *Be Selective.* Prayerfully review the possible applications you have listed in the observation section of your study. Select the one you feel the Holy Spirit would have you work on now. Don't try to choose more than one as this can prove to be counterproductive. If you try to apply too many, you will become frustrated and unable to apply any. It is like someone throwing a dozen eggs to you. Trying to catch them all can cause you to miss them all. Select one, make sure you catch it, and let the rest go by.

The process is subjective simply because it is between you and the Lord. If your heart is open and teachable, He will reveal what He wants you to apply.

4. *Be Specific.* Resist the temptation to address yourself to generalities. Put your finger on the heart of the problem and press.

For example, "Philippians 2:5—'God would have me to be more like Jesus'" is too general.

On the other hand, the following is a more specific way of making an application. "When Paul said that Jesus took on Himself 'the very nature of a servant' (Philippians 2:7), I realized that I have not been serving my family as I should. I sit around and let my wife and children wait on me and find myself resenting it when I have to go out of my way to do anything for them."

5. *Be Personal*. How easy it is to use pronouns such as "we," "us," "they," and "our" when making application. How hard it is to talk in terms of "I," "me," "my," and "mine." This is not "our" problem; it is "my" problem. When writing your applications, stick to the first person singular pronouns.

6. *Write Out Your Application*. As an integral and essential part of your study, the application should be written out. It is hard on pride to verbalize on paper areas of personal application, but you will find it extremely helpful in your quest to do business with God. Writing it out affords an opportunity to go back and check your progress against what you specifically vowed before God you would do.

7. *Set Up a Check-up Procedure*. Sometimes your application will require one specific thing like returning a book you borrowed months before, or apologizing to someone for a wrong you did. At other times your application will require time. It may be a habit God wants you to break, or a series of steps you may have to take like paying installments on a large overdue bill. Then too there will be times when the Holy Spirit will give you a long-range project to work on such as working on an attitude or a virtue.

For example, you are studying the life of Moses and note as a possible application Numbers 12:3, "Now the man Moses was very *meek,* above all the men which were upon the face of the earth." You look up the word *meek* to obtain a precise definition and find it means, "Enduring injury with patience and without resentment" *(Webster's).* The Holy Spirit speaks to you about your unwillingness to let people take advantage of you without a fight. You list specific illustrations when this has been true in your life, but you also realize that a proper application is going to take a major re-working of your attitude.

This type of an application may require a year to work on—not to the exclusion of any further applications during the year—but certainly as the major area on which you will be working. Numerous short-range applications may need to be made throughout the year, but this is the major long-range one.

The longer an application takes, the more difficult it is to check up on the progress. Also, applications dealing with attitudes and motives are harder to measure than those dealing with specific points of action. All of this must be taken into consideration when seeking ways to check up on yourself.

Returning to the application of meekness taken from the life of Moses, a possible plan of attack would be:

- "I will memorize Numbers 12:3 and review it daily throughout the year."
- "I will write *meek* on a card and tape it to the mirror in the bathroom, so that daily I will be reminded of my need to work on this. Each morning I will review Numbers 12:3 and pray about its application in my life for *that* day."
- "I will share this need with my spouse and with [a friend], who knows me well. Once a month I will talk over my progress with them and ask for a frank evaluation."

Example of a Typical Application

Following is an example of an application that might be written from a study of Philippians 3.

The passage—"In my study of Philippians 3 the Holy Spirit convicted me of my gluttony through verses 18-19: 'For, as I have often told you before and now say again even with tears, many live as enemies of the cross of Christ. Their destiny is destruction, their god is their stomach, and their glory is in their shame. Their mind is on earthly things.'"

An example—"The other day we were over to the home of Mrs. Jones for dinner and she had prepared the most delicious fried chicken I had ever seen. I overate totally. I knew at the time I was doing it, and felt uncomfortable and embarrassed afterward. I simply love good food."

The solution—"I must 'put a knife to my throat.' When I eat, especially in the home of another, I will take but *one* helping and a moderate one at that."

The specific steps—"To insure that I follow through on this application, I covenant before God that I will:

"1. During grace before each meal, silently ask the Lord to enable me to eat moderately.

"2. Ask my spouse to kick me under the table each time I become immoderate as a gentle reminder of my vow before God.

"3. Write a note of apology to Mrs. Jones for the way I behaved at her table. This will be hard, but it will reinforce my determination never to do it again."

Summary

By its very nature, an application is a personal thing. The above are suggestions on how you can put "shoe leather" on your desire to apply the Scriptures. The bottom line, however, is a change in your character. This change must originate from within. The Holy Spirit will give you wisdom and the courage of your convictions as you apply His Word.

SECTION

IV Conclusion

17 Summary and Conclusion

It has been one of the aims of this book to provide simple ground rules of interpretation that would lead you to a more accurate and consequently more rewarding Bible study program. Twenty-four rules with half a dozen or so corollaries may seem like a rather large plate of food to digest, but you can do it. Actually much of what we read soon leaves the conscious mind and slips into the subconscious. Only when some related thought or experience triggers what is stored there does it surface to the conscious once again.

As you engage in Bible study (see Sections II and III in the book), the process of interpreting the Scriptures will trigger the thoughts of the first section now stored in your subconscious mind and bring them to the surface. You can refer to the ground rule in question and refresh your memory on its application. Before long, these rules will become almost second nature to you—much like striking the keys of the piano for an accomplished pianist.

To the degree that they are valid, the rules contained in this book should be biblically self-evident. As you read them, they should have appeared obvious. If you entertain the possibility of substituting an alternative for any one of the rules, the implications of such a change should make it unacceptable.

For example, Rule 12 reads, *Interpret a word in relation to its sentence and context.* Let's suggest as an alternative that we *not* interpret a word in light of its context, but solely on the basis of what the dictionary says. Then Paul is referring to four-legged animals when he refers to "dogs" (Philippians 3:2), and King Herod is a literal "fox" (Luke 13:32).

These rules, if they are sound and accurate, conform with the spirit and content of what the Bible states is true.

There may have been a time, say a generation or so ago, when writing out such self-evident rules was unnecessary. But in today's society things have changed; our relativistic generation questions absolutes and blurs issues; and the setting down of rules of interpretation for Bible study has become a necessity. That which is self-evident to a biblically knowledgeable people strikes those unfamiliar with the Bible as new.

This has its good and bad sides. It is a fact that the Scriptures are fresh and alive for the man on the street today. Again and again hungry young men and women are drawn out of relativistic thinking and into an encounter with the dynamic truths of the Bible. That which was embedded in the minds of our forefathers as being "obvious" to the point of being dry is today viewed as new and startling—and that is appealing to people.

The disadvantage is that we have produced a generation of biblical illiterates who not only are unfamiliar with the great truths of the Scriptures, but are unsure of how to go about discovering them. So a basic and simple approach to the principles of biblical interpretation is a great need today.

In seeking to apply these rules you must remember that there is a difference between the rules being biblically correct, and using them properly. A hammer is the correct tool to drive in a nail, but using a hammer does not guarantee that you won't bend the nail. As you apply these rules of interpretation to your Bible study, you are not guaranteed a correct interpretation at every try. You will make mistakes. But hopefully proficiency and accuracy will come with faithful practice.

There may have been times as you read through the chapters in Section I that you felt you were "left hanging" as to what the proper interpretation of a passage should be. Though it was not the intent to leave the reader "hanging," the section did try to keep from interpreting the passages for you.

The goal of Section I has been the establishment of ground rules for interpretation, not interpretation itself. Unfortunately this has not always been possible. Traces of the author's theological bias crept in, though hopefully at a minimum.

Some have suggested a lab session on some of the passages. An exposition of 1 John 2:6-10 on pages 59-60 afforded such an opportunity. Another suggestion was to expound a passage using as many of the ground rules as possible.

These suggestions were appealing, but would no doubt have detracted from the purpose of the section. We would forever be debating whether the right conclusion was drawn from a particular rule. Therefore the meaning of each of the 24 rules was explained, and their application left to you.

Section II gave you five methods of Bible study that enable you to begin applying the rules of interpretation to specific situations. Section III went into greater depth on the way to use the four essential parts of Bible study—observation, interpretation, correlation, and application.

Taken together, these three sections put into your hands a tool for becoming biblically literate and interpreting what you study correctly. That will make you a more useful citizen of the kingdom of God and a more able worker in the church of Jesus Christ.

These last two sections were different from the first in that you have been encouraged to use your own creativity. Pick and choose from that material, remembering that your study of the Bible is simply made up of *observation, interpretation, correlation,* and *application.* There are *rules* for interpreting the Scriptures, but just guidelines in Bible study, for here the approach is much more flexible.

If you feel that you are just a beginner in the art of properly interpreting and studying the Bible, be encouraged to take bold steps forward. Don't fasten your eyes on the possible mistakes you may make, but on the incomparable Christ and the rich potential you have of getting to know Him better.

Appendix

This suggested program is arranged for 45 weeks of study each year. A two-week synthetic study is scheduled for each book of the Bible—an introductory survey study before and a concluding summary study after. (This means that seven weeks are allowed for a five-chapter book like 1 Thessalonians.). *Topical* and *Biographical* studies are *italicized*. The order of topical studies assumes a person has already been fairly well grounded in basic doctrines through question-and-answer studies. Old Testament chapter studies are underlined.

This program is not meant to be a rigid one, and you may adjust it as you feel you need for your own study program. Interchange books, topics, biographies, and Old Testament chapters, adding or deleting as you think best.

First Year

	Weeks
1 Thessalonians	7
1 John	7
Philippians	6
Salvation	2
Witnessing	2
Follow-up	2
Gospel of Mark	18
Biographical: Daniel (Daniel 1–6)	1

Second Year   **Weeks**

Colossians   6
Jesus Christ (deity, death, resurrection)   3
1 Timothy   8
Biographical: Timothy (use a concordance)   1
Gospel of John   23
Prayer   2
Biographical: Josiah (2 Kings 22–23;
     2 Chronicles 34–35)   1
Isaiah 52:13–53:12   1

Third Year

Galatians   8
The Holy Spirit and the Lordship of Christ   3
Ephesians   8
Biographical: Barnabas (use a
    concordance)   1
Romans   18
Exodus 20   1
2 Timothy   6

Fourth Year

The Word of God   2
Titus   5
Biographical: Gideon (Judges 6–8)   1
Obedience   1
Biographical: Joseph (Genesis 28–50)   2
Acts   30
Exodus 12   1
Pacesetting   1
Genesis 3   1
World Vision   1

Fifth Year	**Weeks**
1 Peter	7
Suffering	1
Joshua 1	1
1 Corinthians	18
Biographical: Elijah (1 Kings 17–22;	
2 Kings 1–2)	1
The Will of God	2
Hebrews	15

Sixth Year	
2 Thessalonians	5
Stewardship and Generosity	2
Genesis 22	1
Love	2
Psalm 1	1
The Second Coming of Christ	3
Psalm 2	1
Biographical: Hezekiah (2 Kings 18–20;	
2 Chronicles 29–32; Isaiah 35–39)	2
Gospel of Luke	26
The Church, Church Growth, and Other	
Christian Works	2

Seventh Year	
James	7
The Tongue	1
Temptation and Victory	1
Purity	1
Biographical: Elisha (2 Kings 1–13)	1
2 Peter	5
Repentance	1
Sin	2

	Weeks
Satan	2
Psalm 23	1
Psalm 37	1
2 Corinthians	15
1 Samuel 17	1
2 Samuel 7	1
Discipline and Diligence	1
Good Works	1
Proverbs 2	1
Psalm 78	1
2 John	1

Seven-year Summary:

23 New Testament Books (Mark through 2 John)	249
24 *Topical Studies*	41
9 *Biographical Studies*	11
14 Old Testament Chapters	14
Seven Years at 45 Weeks per Year	315

Eighth Year

3 John	1
Jude	1
Humility	1
Honesty	1
Revelation	24
Judgment and Hell	2
Biographical: Nehemiah (Nehemiah 1–13)	2
Genesis 1	1

	Weeks
Genesis 12	1
Philemon	1
Redeeming the Time	1
Biographical: Peter (use a concordance)	5
Judges 7	1
1 Kings 18	1
Job 1	1
Job 2	1

Ninth Year

	Weeks
Gospel of Matthew	30
Correction and Rebuke	1
2 Kings 17	1
Psalm 40	1
Numbers 14	1
Faithfulness—God's; Man's Required	2
Psalm 103	1
Deuteronomy 4	1
Joshua 3	1
Jonah	6

In the Tenth Year you may begin again, selecting from the previous nine, or you may add any other Old Testament books, topics, and biographies that you desire.